Sloyd

In Great Britain And America
1890 & 1906

Hand-Craft : An English Exposition Of Slöjd
by John D. Sutcliffe
of the Manchester Recreative Evening Classes

1890

Elementary Sloyd And Whittling
By Gustaf Larsson
Principal of the Sloyd Training School
Boston, Massachusetts

1906

Edited by Gary Roberts

The Toolemera Press
History Preserved
www.toolemerapress.com

Slojd In Great Britain And America: 1890 & 1906

No part of this book may be reproduced, stored in an electronic retrieval system, or transmitted in any form or by an means, electronic, mechanical, photocopy, photographic or otherwise without the written permission of the publisher.

Excerpts of one page or less for the purposes of review and comment are permissible.

Copyright © 2019 The Toolemera Press
All rights reserved.

International Standard Book Number
ISBN-13: 978-1-0878-0625-9
(Trade Paper)

Published by
The Toolemera Press
Wilmington, North Carolina
USA 28401

Manufactured in the United States of America

www.toolemerapress.com

Introduction by Otto Salomon: from *Practical Directions For Making The High School Series of Slojd Models. 1892*

There is perhaps no more dangerous attitude of mind than that of the people whose opinions remain stationary. Everything, so far at all events as regards the outward form, is subject to the laws of change and development. That which was admirably adapted for the past, may be unsuitable for the present, and entirely useless in the future. We may admit this general truth without committing ourselves to the propositions that everything old is bad and that everything new is good. There are truths which hold good for all time, and which, at the outside, merely assume a different form of expression at different periods; while many new doctrines at first sight satisfactory, prove insufficient when tested by experience.

It is especially important in educational matters, that we should understand how to steer the middle course between conservative spirit which is identical with surrender to the enemy of all progress - "use and want," and the nervous, restless search after novelty which is ever replacing one imperfectly tested method by another equally untried. The zealous teacher must always bear in mind that, while is work in both form and spirit should bear the impress of development, this development must be gradual and well-considered. The older he is and the greater the stores of experience at his command, the more clearly will he apprehend that the whole question of education is much more complicated than he at first imagined it to be. Much that on superficial observation seemed simple and clear, on closer inspection turns out to be the result of many and complex factors. The experienced teacher therefore guards against hasty conclusions regarding the merits of particular educational methods. Not content with seeing them in operation, he studies them, and before abandoning one and adopting another, he seeks assurance that the new method is not only newer but better than the old. He knows too well that what promises well in theory, does not always stand the test of practice.

Toolemera Press
History Preserved
www.toolemerapress.com

HAND-CRAFT:

THE MOST RELIABLE BASIS OF TECHNICAL EDUCATION IN SCHOOLS AND CLASSES.

A TEXT BOOK

EMBODYING A SYSTEM OF PURE MECHANICAL ART, WITHOUT THE AID OF MACHINERY; BEING AN ENGLISH EXPOSITION OF

SLÖJD

AS CULTIVATED IN SWEDEN, AND GENERALLY ADOPTED BY ALL SCANDINAVIAN PEOPLES, TO THEIR GREAT ADVANTAGE.

EXPLAINED AND ILLUSTRATED

BY

JOHN D. SUTCLIFFE,
OF THE MANCHESTER RECREATIVE EVENING CLASSES.

WITH AN INTRODUCTION BY
T. C. HORSFALL, J.P.

GRIFFITH FARRAN OKEDEN & WELSH
NEWBERY HOUSE
CHARING CROSS ROAD LONDON
AND AT SYDNEY
1890

(The rights of translation and of reproduction are reserved.)

INTRODUCTION.

IT is surprising that so few efforts have hitherto been made in this country to introduce manual training into Elementary Schools. Adequate reason for making such training part of the national system of education exists in the fact, that a large proportion of the people have to earn their livelihood by industries for the attainment of a high degree of skill in which early training of hand and eye is as necessary as it is for success in the use of musical instruments. There can be no doubt that if, in 1870, a system, resembling that of Sloyd, had been generally introduced into English Elementary Schools, the joiners, metal-workers, and most other craftsmen of to-day, would possess more skill in their own work, and more interest in all kinds of manual work, than they do now possess, and that English workpeople, finding that their children received at school kinds of training obviously well fitted to increase wage-earning power, would less commonly than now be careless with regard to their children's attendance at school.

This reason for desiring the introduction of manual training into Elementary Schools might have been expected to suggest itself to all persons who are acquainted with the conditions under which the mass of English people live; but experience gained in Sweden and other countries where the Sloyd system has been largely used, proves that there are also strong educational reasons for desiring that Sloyd shall be introduced into all English Elementary Schools as soon as possible. It has been found that this admirably graduated system of training not only fosters deftness of hand and correctness of eye, as it might be expected to do, but also has distinctly moral and intellectual effects, as it promotes patient attention, steady application, and interest in work, to a very high degree.

Its effect on many of the large class of children who, though not dullards, show lack of interest in, and deficiency in the power to understand, the subjects comprised in the ordinary school-curriculum, has been most beneficial. In their Sloyd-lessons many of these children have found themselves the equals, some more than the equals, of companions far their superiors at book-work, and have by this gained a confidence in their own ability which has often reacted on their power and their will to conquer their other lessons. Thus many children who, when they first began Sloyd, were distinctly below the average in intelligence, have become under its influence completely "normal." On nearly all children the effect of this kind of training has been so vivifying that, at least, as much progress has been made with other subjects, when several hours weekly have been given to Sloyd, as had been made previously when all the school-time was given to them. The general educational value of Sloyd has, indeed, been found to be so great, that in some schools in Swedish towns as many as eight hours are given to it each week.

All persons who know how badly prepared are the majority of the children who now leave our Elementary Schools for gaining rapidly skill in the work by which they have to live, or for taking an intelligent interest in their own work or in the best handiwork of others, most strongly desire that the educational authorities in this country will no longer delay the introduction of a system, the great usefulness of which has been so fully ascertained in other lands, and for which many well-trained English teachers can now be obtained. Mr Sutcliffe brought to the careful study of Sloyd, knowledge of the methods of wood-carving; and his treatise will doubtless be found to be helpful to all teachers of the new system.

T. C. HORSFALL, J.P.

SWANSCOE PARK,
near MACCLESFIELD.

NOTE BY THE AUTHOR.

SOME friends have advised that elementary suggestions should have been given as guidance for the use of the tools. Everything of the kind has been omitted, because it is vain to rely upon book knowledge in such matters. How to handle and use the tools can only be well imparted by a competent teacher in practice. The author avails himself of two more lines, wherein to acknowledge the valuable literary assistance he has received from his friend, Mr Richard Russell, of Ashbourne House, Herne Hill, London.   J. D. S.

PENDLETON, MANCHESTER,
March 1890.

HAND-CRAFT.

FOR some generations there has been cultivated in Sweden, and amongst Scandinavian and kindred peoples, a course of training in personal ingenuity, unknown in most other countries. It does not seem to have ever been persevered in after the manner of trading industry, but as a means of promoting throughout the community a taste and skill for the performance of highly-finished productions in mechanical art, proceeding from the simple to the complex, and resulting in a widely-diffused facility for all kinds of constructive occupations.

Such course or system of training is called Sloyd, and written Slöjd. For the majority of English people such a word cannot have a meaning, and cannot appeal with adequate force to popular appreciation. The nearest equivalent in English to the Swedish word Slöjd would seem to be Hand-Craft, or mechanical training for the hand, undertaken voluntarily for the satisfaction of acquiring manual skill in general, as distinguished from a handicraft of limited application, pursued of necessity from day to day, rather by routine than by skill.

Hand-Craft is therefore adopted as synonymous in England with the word Slöjd in Sweden.

As cultivated in Sweden, it involves all kinds of manual

training, and is applicable to highly finished productions in leather, metal, and various other substances, but it suffices, for educational purposes, to limit teaching and exercise to objects made of wood.

It must always be borne in mind that Hand-Craft is mainly educational, and is valuable, not for what it produces, but for the training which the production involves; just as the letters of the alphabet, and their accurate use, are the essential preliminaries to literary attainments. It imparts and cultivates mechanical dexterity, just as learning to read and write spontaneously developes mental capacity. Therefore, whoever masters a course of Hand-Craft acquires an aptitude for all kinds of material processes. Such an aptitude, while useful and gratifying to the individual, is of the greatest consequence amongst people so deeply interested as the English are in manufacturing pursuits.

Hand-Craft also has strong claims to be cultivated as a recreation, and experience proves that it may be so regarded, with every prospect of becoming popular as such.

Touching this matter of recreation, and those who have not the faculty for viewing the subject in that light, reference may be made to familiar facts with reference to chess. Perhaps there is nothing that, to the uninitiated, appears more stupid, insipid, and purposeless than the progress of that game. Yet there are thousands, who have so regarded it, who, after being well initiated, have become interested and absorbed by it, to an extent exceeding the possibilities of their original belief.

So it is with Hand-Craft, with this difference, that Hand-Craft, while supplying an incentive to wholesome perseverance, developing into a fascinating recreation, is suggestive at every turn of life-long utility, with reference to an infinite variety of probable subsequent experience. It promotes a delightful consciousness of the merits of neat, natty tastefulness and judgment with reference to every material thing, and trains the mind and the eye, as well as the hand, to perceive and appreciate excellence of design and finish, proportion, beauty, and adaptability of the most familiar appliances.

Training of this kind has, in recent years, been much stimulated by the establishment of an Institute or Seminary for its teaching and cultivation at Nääs in Sweden, where very generous accommodation and facilities are provided for the instruction of teachers from all parts of Sweden and the rest of the world. The subsequent mission of each of those teachers is to diffuse the taste and knowledge he has thus acquired amongst his own people on his return to them, or amongst other people where he may find encouragement to settle for that purpose.

Thus have the foundations been laid for this genial drawing out and exercise of latent mechanical genius amongst the people of England. With the object of widening those foundations, these pages have been prepared; primarily as forming a Text Book for Teachers, but also as an incentive to parents, educationists, and statesmen to fortify the rising generation of England against the opprobrium so justly alleged against the English of the present day, that they are behind the rest of the industrial world in those elements of mechanical taste and skill, which are becoming more and more essential to the maintenance of manufacturing and commercial prosperity.

An earnest determination to promote amendment in these respects cannot be better carried into effect than by insisting that Hand-Craft shall be regarded as an essential branch of the Technical Education that is now struggling to assert itself usefully. If such a branch be left out, the mere teaching of routine trade processes will inevitably fail. Such routine processes are many of them in heavy-handed, rough disregard of the nicety, accuracy, finish, and judgment which intelligent exercise in Hand-Craft can alone impart; which is the only reliable basis for the superior mechanical results so much needed.

Hand-Craft in wood is distinguished from carpentry or joinery in many important respects.

There is no division of labour.

Everything produced is the entire work of one operator, for the defects of which he is solely responsible.

This directness of responsibility is one of the great merits of Hand-Craft, being calculated to promote wholesome pride in the excellence of complete work; a sentiment that is apt to be very weak, or totally wanting, where division of labour is much relied upon.

The intellectual faculties are brought into unison with the

hand, by knowledge and experience developing together with increasing dexterity.

Genuine respect and sympathy are developed for manual toil by familiarity with its application.

Love of work in general is developed, and a taste for it instilled by practical experience of its utility.

Habits of attention, perseverance, industry, and discipline are formed, cultivated, and unconsciously grafted upon the pupil, by the application necessary to excel.

Independence, order, and cleanliness spontaneously grow and become part of the nature of the operator.

Manual dexterity being thoroughly established, the operator is endowed with the consequent acquired ability for dealing with the practical business of life.

Education being the object that should be constantly kept in view, in the teaching and practice of Hand-Craft, it should be thoroughly appreciated that it is adapted for forming and shaping the entire bent of all the faculties.

The objects recommended to work upon are all small, and are therefore within the capacity of the very young, and of both sexes.

For the same reason, the eye, the hand, and the judgment are trained to precise form and finish in the minutest details. This is important, for, though it is generally easier to make something large and rough than small and smooth, no one who is incapable of making a small model well can make a large one any better.

Small objects are invariably the best training to work upon, as being certain to inspire appreciation for neatness, exactness, and accuracy.

BASIS OF TEACHING.

Practical teaching of Hand-Craft is based upon models for imitation.

These models, distinguished by numbering from 1A and 1B to 25, are represented by the drawings accompanying these pages, and the instructions hereafter subjoined are explained by reference to the drawings.

The following is a

LIST OF THE MODELS.

₊ The second column indicates the kind of wood required— B. signifying Beech or Birch, and F. signifying Fir, commonly called Deal or Pine; the class of wood usually distinguished as Pine being preferable to the rougher-grained wood generally classed as Deal.

No.	Wood.	Names of Models.
1A.	B.	Kindergarten Pointer.
1B.	B.	Another variety of the same.
2.	B.	Parcel-Pin or Carrier.
3.	F.	Flower-Stick.

HAND-CRAFT.

No.	Wood.	Names of Models.
4.	B.	Envelope Opener.
5.	F.	Rectangular Flower-Stick.
6.	F.	Pencil Holder.
7.	F.	Key Label.
8.	B.	Thread-Winder.
9.	F.	Dibble for the Garden.
10.	B.	Pen-Rest.
11.	F.	Flower-pot Stand.
12.	B.	Paper-Knife.
13.	B.	Knife-Rest.
14.	B.	Bowl, for Toilette, &c.
15.	B.	Hammer Handle.
16.	B.	Handle for Chisel or File.
17.	B.	Spoon.
18.	F.	Chopping-Board.
19.	B.	Measure (Half-yard).
20.	B.	Scoop for Flour, Sugar, &c.
21.	F.	Hanging-Pegs.
22.	F.	Stand for Flower-Pot, &c.
23.	F.	Footstool.
24.	F. & B.	Book Carrier.
25.	B.	Ladle.

TOOLS AND APPLIANCES.

The following is a List of Tools and Appliances necessary for producing the models before enumerated, with the cost of each, both Swedish and English.

Descriptions of Articles.	Best Swedish.		Best English.	
	s.	d.	s.	d.
Carpenter's Bench in Pine, 6 ft. long	11	3	13	0
Knife (resembling a Shoemaker's)	0	4	0	8
Two Frame Saws, blades ¾ and 1¼ wide	2	7*	10	6
Tenon or Dovetail Saw (small)	2	0	3	0
Jack Plane	1	8	4	9
Smooth Plane	1	1	3	9
Three Furmer Chisels, ⅜, ¾, and 1¼ wide	1	2	2	4
Three Outside Gouges, ½, ⅞, and 1⅛ wide	1	4	2	8
Two-foot Rule	0	6	0	6
Square (6 in.)	1	6	1	10
Bevel (6 in.)	0	8	2	3
Marking Gauge	0	6	0	6
Compasses	1	0	1	8
Hammer (small)	0	8	0	8
Mallet	0	6	1	0
Carry forward,	26	9	49	1

* Nothing exactly like this Swedish Saw is made in England.

HAND-CRAFT.

Description of Articles.	Best Swedish.		Best English.	
	s.	d.	s.	d.
Brought forward,	26	9	49	1
Oilstone	0	7	1	0
Scraper, with round end	0	2	0	5
Two Files (half round), one rough, the other smooth	1	0	3	0
Chopper or Axe	1	10	1	6
Spokeshave (iron)	0	5	1	0
Screw-driver	0	3	0	7
Glue-Pot and Brush	1	6	0	10
Pincers	0	7	0	9
Two Brad-Awls	0	2	0	4
Brace and twenty-four Bits	4	0	6	9
Sand-paper No. 1A				
Pencil				
*	37	3	65	3

Although the prices of the English tools are so much higher than the Swedish (with few exceptions), they are cheaper in the end. They are more carefully made; the wood is drier and better selected; and Swedish steel is not to be compared with English. At the same time, the Swedish tools are good enough to put into the hands of school boys and girls, and they have also the advantage of being considerably lighter in weight.

* Exclusive of carriage from Gothenburg.

THE BENCH.

A drawing of the Bench is annexed, to show the difference between one adapted for Sloyd or Hand-Craft and the kind in common use by carpenters. The Sloyd Bench is usually about 7 ft. long, 2 ft. wide, and 3 ft. 3 in. high. As shown in the drawing, it has an extra Bench Screw at the end, which enables the student to fix a piece of level wood rigidly on the top of the Bench, by placing the end against a Stop, as shown in the drawing, and bringing the pressure of the End Screw to bear on the other end. The numerous holes (shown in the drawing) on the Bench Top, are so arranged that the Stop can be fixed in any of them. For school work the Benches are often made double—that is, with a Screw on each side and on each end of the Bench. This arrangement economises space, and answers all practical purposes; enabling two students to work at one bench. The Sloyder will find it an advantage to fix a small drawer under the bench top. In this he should keep his sandpaper and files, as nothing is so detrimental to the edges of the sharp tools as these two articles.

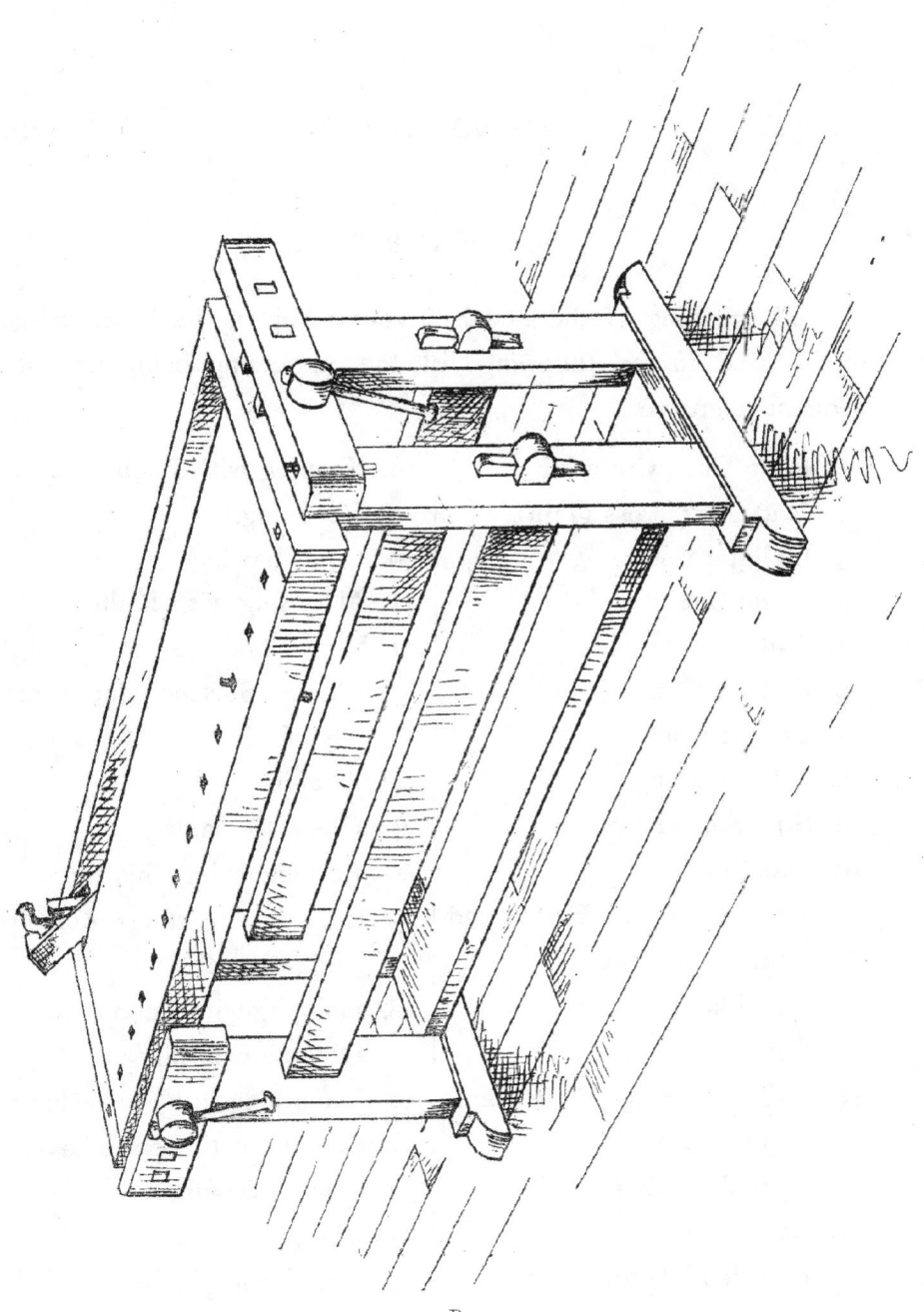

B

TOOL EXERCISES.

The making of the models involves training in the exercises enumerated in the following list, the numbering being for subsequent reference.

1. Long Cut (with grain).
2. End Cut (across grain).
3. Oblique Cut.
4. Bevel Cut.
5. Sawing off.
6. Convex Cut.
7. Long Sawing.
8. Edge Planing.
9. Squaring with Set Square.
10. Gauging.
11. Drilling with Brace and Shell-Bit.
12. Flat Planing.
13. Filing.
14. Drilling with Brace and Centre-Bit.
15. Curved Sawing.
16. Concave Cut.
17. Bevelled Planing.
18. Shaping with Plane.
19. Chopping.
20. Cross-Sawing,
21. Mortising with Knife.
22. Wave-Sawing.
23. Plane Surface-Cut with Knife.
24. Scraping.
25. Obstacle-Planing.
26. Perpendicular Chiselling.
27. Concave Chiselling or Gouging.
28. Gouging with Spoon-Iron.
29. Oblique Chiselling.
30. Smoothing with Spokeshave.
31. Shaping with Spokeshave.
32. Oblique Sawing.
33. Oblique Planing.
34. End Planing.

35. Exercises with Smoothing Plane.
36. Work in Hard Wood.
37. Dowelling or Round Mortising.
38. Bevelling Edge with Plane Oblique.
39. Gluing.
40. Sinking in of Iron Plates.
41. Nailing.
42. Sinking of Nails.
43. Bevelling with Shaping Knife.
44. Perpendicular Gouging.
45. Point Planing.
46. Oblique Grooving.
47. Circular Sawing.
48. Fixing with Screws.
49. Modelling with Knife.

MAKING OF THE MODELS.

The following are the descriptions of how to apply the Exercises to the making of the Models.

No. 1A. Kindergarten Pointer.

(Requiring Exercises 1 and 2.)

Commence with a piece of Beech, rather more than 5 in. long, and not less than ¾ in. thick. It is all the better, for this and other exercises, if it is split from a larger piece, and has no side either square or straight. With the knife, make one side level and smooth, to a width rather exceeding ⅜ in. When that is done perfectly, make another straight side at right angles to the first. Trim the ends; then mark with the pencil at each end a ⅜-in.

square, with the two straight sides as bases. Then cut two additional straight sides in unison with those squares. This will produce a stem a shade more than 5 in. long and $\frac{3}{8}$ in. square. Mark each end with a diagram thus ⊠; then draw corresponding lines along each side. Then, letting one end remain the same size; reduce the other end to $\frac{1}{8}$ in. square (as shown in centre of diagram) by tapering each side symmetrically throughout. This will result in the stem being $\frac{3}{8}$ in. square at one end and $\frac{1}{8}$ in. square at the other end. Then, guided by the diagram at the thicker end, take off the four corners symmetrically throughout, thus producing a tapered octagonal stem. Then, in like manner, take off the eight corners with great precision, so as to maintain uniform symmetry, and the result will be a tapered stem, approximately round throughout and pointed at one end.

The Long Cut having, thus far, been solely resorted to, measure from the point, and make a mark at 4 in.; then cut off at the mark, thus exercising the Cross Cut. Then, by judiciously applying sand-paper, the pointer may be made perfectly smooth and almost perfectly round, as it should be throughout.

No. 1B. KINDERGARTEN POINTER.
(Requiring Exercises 1, 2, and 3.)

Proceed as for the previous model until the round pointer is produced. Then apply Exercise 3 to the two Oblique Cuts shown from *A* to *a* in the figures 1, 2, and 3, of drawings No. 1B. These Oblique Cuts demand great care and precision, as the Cuts should be precisely opposite each other, perfectly level and symmetrical.

No. 2. Parcel-Pin or Carrier.
(Requiring Exercises 1, 2, and 4.)

Commence with a piece of Beech rather more than 3 in. long and ⅝ in. thick. Reduce it in like manner as previously described to a stem 3 in. long and ⅜ in. square throughout. Then apply Exercise 4, and so bevel the sides and ends as to make chamfers, as shown in Figs. 1, 2, and 3 of drawings No. 2. Then draw a line across the centre of one side, and there cut a V-shaped notch as shown in Figs. 1 and 2, so as to provide for a string. Then finish with a piece of sand-paper laid upon a flat surface, upon which first rub the sides, then the chamfers, and lastly the ends.

No. 3. Flower-Stick.
(Requiring Exercises 5, 1, 2, and 6.)

This is the first model made in soft wood, and introduces Exercise 5, Sawing Off. From the edge of a ¾-in. board saw off a piece the same width as the thickness, and about 14 in. long. Proceed as for No. 1A until a rod is produced ½ in. square throughout. Then, by a cross made from corner to corner ⊠ find

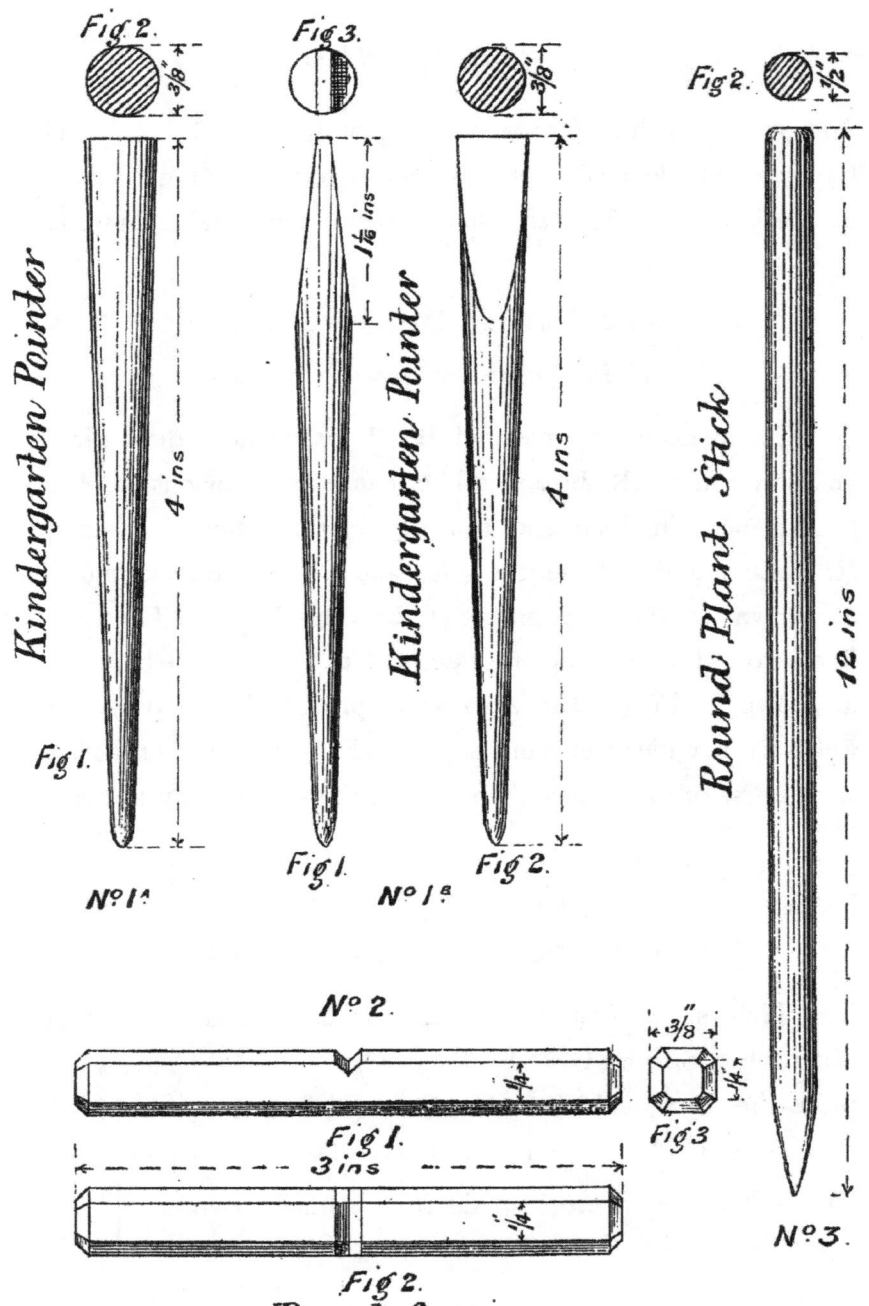

the centre of one end. Then take off the corners throughout until an octagonal rod is produced; then take off the eight corners so as to make the rod round and the same thickness throughout. Then apply Exercise 6, the Convex Cut, and point the end where the centre is marked. Then measure from the point and mark at 12 in., and there cut off at right angles. Then apply sand-paper, and the result will be a tapered symmetrical round rod, pointed at one end, as shown in drawings No. 3.

No. 4. ENVELOPE OPENER.

(Requiring Exercises 5, 1, 2, and 6.)

Saw from Beech, a piece about 8 in. long, ¾ in. wide and ½ in. thick. With the knife, make one of the flat sides perfectly level and smooth throughout, and cut one end across at right angles. With a fine pencil, draw on the level side the outline of Fig 1 of drawings No. 4, and also, with compasses, describe on the end the semicircle shown by Fig 3 of drawings No. 4, with the flat edge for the base. Apply the long cut to the edges at right angles to the flat side. Then, on each of the edges thus flattened, draw a line showing the course of the tapering illustration on the first side of Fig. 2 of drawings No. 4. Apply the long cut to each of those lines, at right angles to the edges. This will produce a rod, flat on one side, and presenting a tapered half square on the other. Then shave off the corners of that square, so as to produce half a tapered octagon; then shave off the corners of that octagon, being careful that the work is in unison with the semicircle previously described on the thick end. When so far done to satisfaction, round both ends symmetrically, as shown in Figs. 1 and 2 of drawings No. 4, and finish with sand-paper.

No. 5. Rectangular Flower-Stick, with Chamfered or Bevelled Corners.

(Requiring Exercises 5, 7, 8, 9, 6, and 3.)

In this model the Jack Plane and the Try Square are used for the first time. Saw off from Pine a piece about 16 in. long and ¾ in. square. Plane one side straight and true, and one of the other sides at right angles. Cut each end across at right angles, and on each end, using the planed edges as basis, mark Fig. 2 of drawings No. 5. Then plane the other two sides at right angles, so as to produce a square rod, which, at every part throughout its length, should fit the try square. Then, with the plane, take about two shavings off each corner, in unison with the figures at the ends. Then, with the knife, cut the point from *a* to *a* as shown in Fig. 1 of drawings No. 5. Then measure from the long-pointed end, mark the exact length, cut across at the mark, and cut the other end to a point with eight sides as shown in Figs. 1 and 2. Finish with sand-paper at the long-pointed end only.

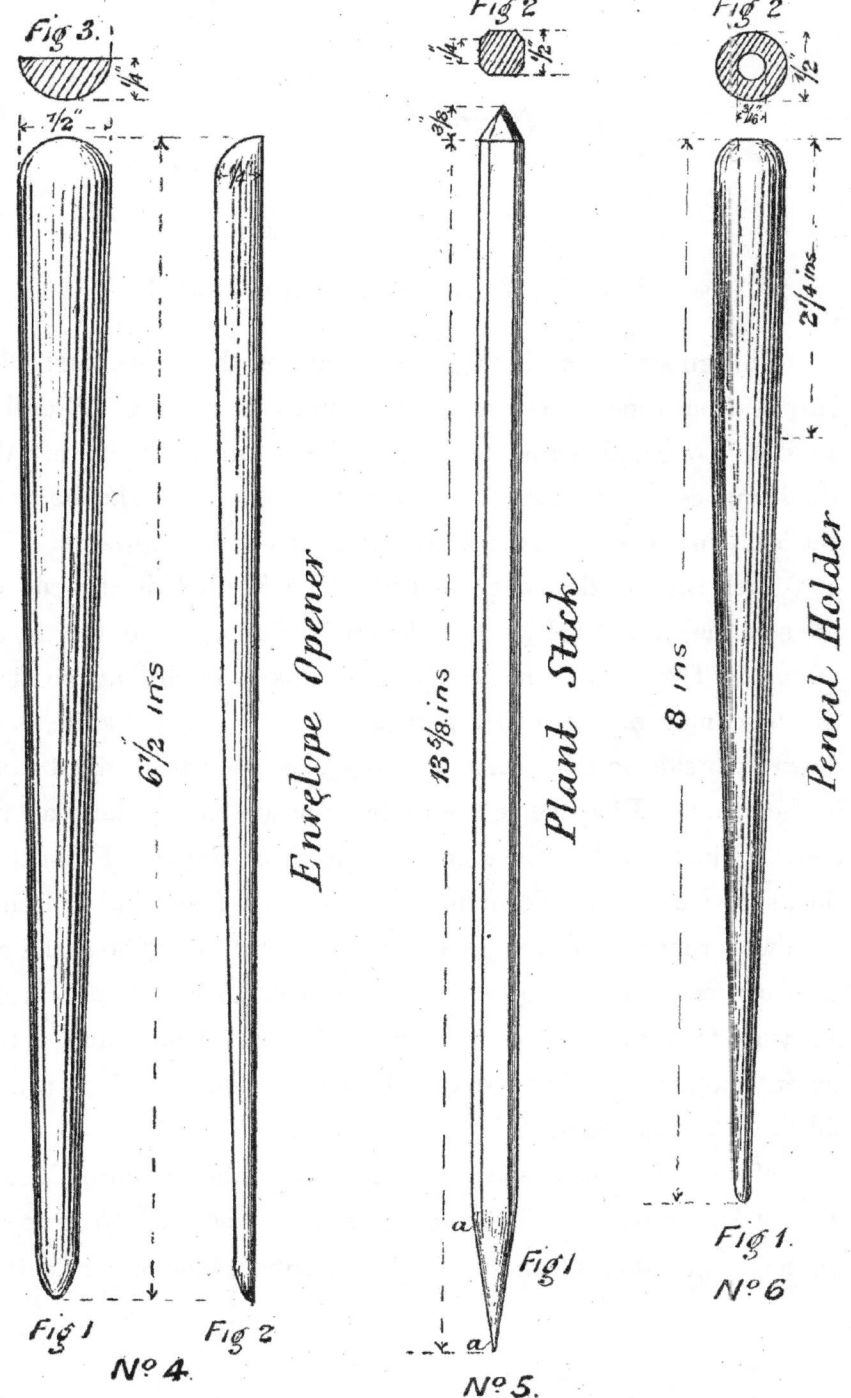

No. 6. Pencil Holder.

(Requiring Exercises 5, 1, 11, 6, and 2.)

This model for the first time introduces the Brace and Bit. Saw off from Pine a piece 10 in. long, and ¾ in. square. With the knife, cut one end across at right angles, and make it smooth. Find the centre of the end as for model No. 1. Fix the stem vertically in the Bench Screw, with the smooth end upwards. Fit a $\frac{3}{16}$-Shell-Bit into the Brace, and bore a centre hole in the end of the stem as shown in Fig. 2 of drawings No. 6, and to the depth dotted in Fig. 1. Great care must be taken in drilling, so that the hole may be clean and perpendicular. With the knife, pare down each side so as to leave a ½-in. square, with the drilled hole in the centre. Find the centre in the opposite end. Mark a line about $2\frac{1}{4}$ in. from the drilled end, as shown in Fig. 1. From that line, shave each side down to the centre last found. Then take off the corners so as to make a tapered octagon. Then take off the corners of the octagon, so as to produce a round tapered rod. Measure from the thick end and mark the exact length, and, at the mark, cut across. Then round the end as shown in Fig. 1, and finish with sand-paper.

NOTE.—This is a repetition to a considerable extent of Model 1 on a larger scale. The student may be tempted to proceed without going through the processes described, but the temptation should be rigorously resisted, as a satisfactory result cannot be obtained except by adhering to all the details prescribed.

No. 7. Key Label.

(Requiring Exercises 5, 12, 8, 9, 10, 11, 6, 2, and 13.)

This is mainly intended for an exercise in planing, and it is better to get out a piece of Pine sufficient for two models—that is, about 9 in. long, $1\frac{3}{4}$ in. wide, and 1 in. thick.

Plane one side, and then one edge, perfectly straight and square to each other. Then set the gauge to $1\frac{1}{2}$ in. to fit Fig. 1 of drawings No. 7. Apply the gauge to the straightened edge and mark off the width along the smooth side. Then plane that edge down to the line so made, using the try-square to keep the edge at right angles with the straightened side. Next find the centre $\frac{3}{4}$ in. from the top end, as shown in Fig. 1. From that centre describe with the compasses a semicircle. Then fit a $\frac{3}{16}$-Shell-bit into the Brace, and bore a hole, at the centre of the semicircle, right through. Then set the gauge to $\frac{5}{16}$ in. for the thickness, as shown by Fig. 2. Apply the gauge to the straightened side, and mark the line for thickness along each edge. Then plane the rough side down to those lines. Then, with the knife, cut round precisely to the semicircle, using the try-square frequently.

[If a double length is commenced with, as before recommended, the centering, marking, drilling, and rounding must be done at both ends.]

Measure from the rounded end, and rule with the square, the length of 4¼ in. Then, with Tenon or Dovetail Saw, cut off just outside the line. Then, with the knife, pare down to the line, and with a file, smooth that end as well as the rounded end, finishing throughout with sand-paper.

No. 8. Thread-Winder.

(Requiring Exercises 5, 7, 12, 8, 9, 10, 14, 15, 1, 6, 16, and 13.)

Beech is required, about 7 in. long, 3 in. wide, and ½ in. thick. Plane one side and one edge. Draw the centre line *A* to *B* in Fig. 1 of drawings No. 8. With square and compasses draw all the other lines shown in the same Fig. Then fit a ¾ in. Centre-bit to the Brace, and bore two holes, one at *A* and the other at *B*. Then, with the smaller turning saw, cut the two outside curved edges as shown in Fig. 1. With the knife, trim to the lines, making the edges square, as shown in Fig. 3. Then shave and slightly round each semicircle, as shown in Figs. 1 and 2, smoothing the edges with the file. Then set the Marking Gauge to ¼ in., and, with the smooth side for a base, mark gauge lines on each edge for thickness, and plane the rough side down to those lines. Then set the plane very fine and take a shaving off the face side so as to remove the pencil and compass marks. Then finish with sand-paper.

No. 9. Dibble for Garden.

(Requiring Exercises 5, 7, 8, 9, 10, 17, 18, 6, 2, and 13.)

Saw out from Fir a piece 14 in. long and 1¼ in. square. Plane one side straight and another side at right angles. Set the Marking Gauge to 1 in., and with the planed side as base, mark lines for thickness along each planed side. Then plane the rough sides down to those lines, using the Try Square frequently. Then, at each end find the centre thus ⊠ with additional lines showing octagons thus ⊠. With the Marking Gauge draw lines from end to end of each side corresponding with the corners of each octagon. Plane the corners of the square down to those octagon lines, thus producing an octagonal rod, and completing the first exercise in bevel planing. Plane off the corners of the octagon throughout, thus producing a rod approximately round, shown in Fig. 2 of drawings No. 9, and so completing the first exercise in shaping with plane. Measure from one end for the point as shown in Fig. 1, and, with the knife, cut the point as roundly and symmetrically as possible, referring to the centre marked at the end as a guide for the precise place of the point. Then measure from the point and mark at 12 in. Cut across at that mark, and round the blunt end thus made, as shown at top of Fig. 1. With the file, dress the end and stray angles throughout, and finish with sand-paper.

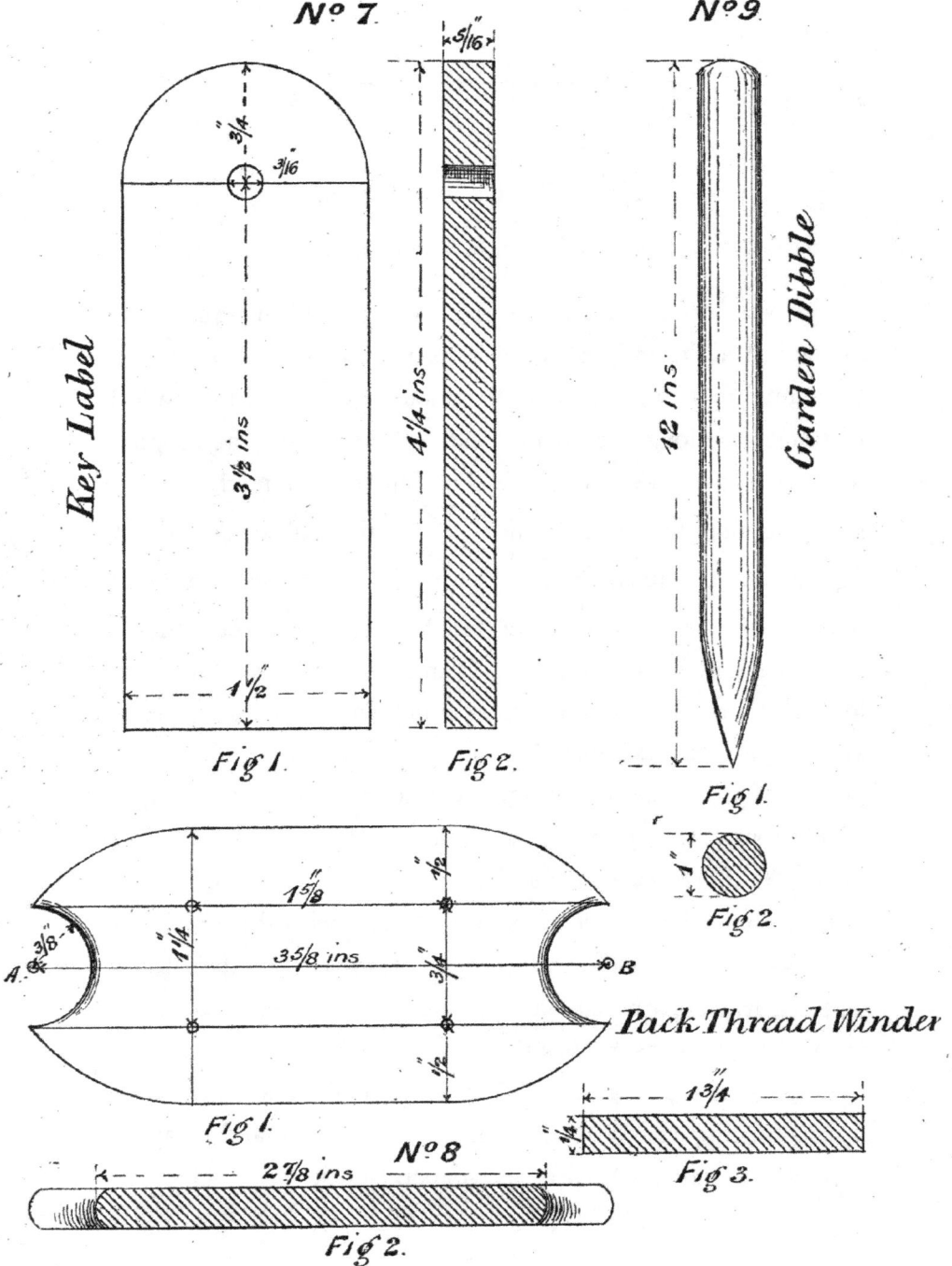

No. 10. Pen Rest.

(Requiring Exercises 5, 8, 9, 10, 20, 1, 2, 18, and 13.)

Cut from Beech a piece 5 in. long, 1 in. wide, and $\frac{3}{4}$ in. thick. Plane one side and one edge at right angles, then gauge and plane to thickness and height, as shown in Fig. 2 of drawings No. 10, but flat on all sides. Saw across both ends at right angles, so as to reduce the length to $3\frac{1}{2}$ in. Select one edge as the top, and, with the square, rule a central line from *e* to *e*, and a line across at each of the places marked *a*, *b*, *c*, and *d* in Fig. 1, continuing each line down both sides. Then, at each end, mark the central place represented by the dot in Fig. 2. From each of those central places describe the semicircle shown at top of Fig. 2. Then mark a line from end to end on each side half way between the top and the bottom.

Then, with the knife, and working to the semicircle at each end, take off the corners of the top, so making half an octagon, and, by taking off the corners of the half octagon, produce a top corresponding to the semicircle at each end, as shown in Fig. 2, taking care that the top of the semicircle throughout centres to the line previously drawn from *e* to *e*. Then, with the tenon saw, at each of the places marked *a*, *b*, *c*, and *d*, saw across a right angle slit $\frac{2}{16}$ in. deep. Then, with the knife or a chisel, cut out the space shown in Fig. 1 from *a* to *b* and from *c* to *d*, taking care that the side of each space is true and square. Then, with the file, round each base as shown at the top of the shaded section in Fig. 2. Then smooth with the file where required, and finish with sand-paper.

No. 11. Flower-Pot Stand.

(Requiring Exercises 5, 7, 8, 9, 10, 2, 1, 6, 13, and 21.)

This consists of two pieces, as shown in Figs. 1 and 2 of drawings No. 11, each piece so made as to cross and fit the other at the centre, hence called a Flower-Pot Cross, the whole being a test of exactness and good work, surpassing any preceding model.

Cut from Pine a piece 12 in. long, 1¼ in. wide, and ½ in. thick. Plane one side and one edge at right angles; then gauge for height and thickness, and plane the other side and edge as shown by the section represented in Fig. 3. Saw across the middle so as to make two pieces, and, from the end of each so cut, measure off and saw both to the equal length of 5¼ in. each, taking care that both ends of each are accurate right angles. Then place them on their sides and draw the centre line indicated by $A B$, continuing the line all round each piece. From the centre, mark off the places indicated by $e f$ and $g h$. At c and d of each, with the compasses, describe the quarter circle shown at each top corner of the figures, striking the segments from the respective dots shown for the purpose near each top corner. Then, with the bottom edge for a base, draw a gauge line on each side of both pieces to the depth represented by ij, and with the tenon saw, make a slit at e and f to the depth of such gauge line. Then, with the knife or chisel, cut out the openings between e and f to the depth of the gauge line, taking care to finish the opening perfectly level and true. Then, at the bottom of one piece and the top of the other, as shown in Figs. 1 and 2, gauge, saw, and cut out the spaces from g to h in the same manner as for the spaces before mentioned. The openings from g to h, if well done, will fit accurately in all directions, and, when put together, will form a firm cross. Then, with the knife, round the corners of each piece, at c and d. Then smooth with file where required, and finish with sand-paper.

No. 13. Knife Rest.*

(Requiring Exercises 5, 7, 8, 9, 10, 20, 18, 26, 1, 2, 27, 13, and 24.)

Cut from Beech a piece about 5 in. long, 1 in. wide, and $\frac{7}{8}$ in. thick. Plane one side and one edge at right angles. Then saw across one end at right angles, and, measuring from that end, mark off the length at $4\frac{1}{4}$ in., and saw off that end at the mark, taking care to maintain right angles. Then gauge and plane the rough side and rough edge to a width of $\frac{7}{8}$ in. and a thickness of $\frac{5}{8}$ in. Then choose one edge for the top, and,

---

* No. 12 (Paper Knife) appears, for convenience of illustration, on page 41, but it should be proceeded with before No. 13.

along the centre of that edge, draw a line from *c* to *c*, as shown in Fig. 1 of drawings No. 13, and continue the line to the extremities of both ends. Then, in manner described for No. 10, gauge, slit, and cut out with chisel the spaces shown in the same Fig. 1 of drawings No. 13, from *a* to *a* and *b* to *b*. Then, with compasses, as indicated in the same Fig., describe on both sides of each top corner, the segment of a circle represented in each case from *c* to *d*. Then, for the first time, resort to Concave Chiselling, and with a broad chisel cut away the corners down to the segments previously described. This process requires great care and judgment. Fix one end of the work upwards in the bench screw, with the top side nearest to the operator, and, after taking off the corner to a considerable extent, with the bevelled side of the chisel towards the wood, shave small pieces away until the segment marks are reached, taking care to keep the whole curve at right angles to the sides throughout, Then, turn the work, and dress the corner at the other end in like manner. Then file judiciously where required, and finish with sand-paper.

Pen Rest.

Fig 1

Fig 2.

Nº 10

Flower Pot Cross.

Fig 1.

Fig 2.

Nº 11.

Fig 3.

Knife Rest.

Fig 1.

Nº 13.

Fig 2.

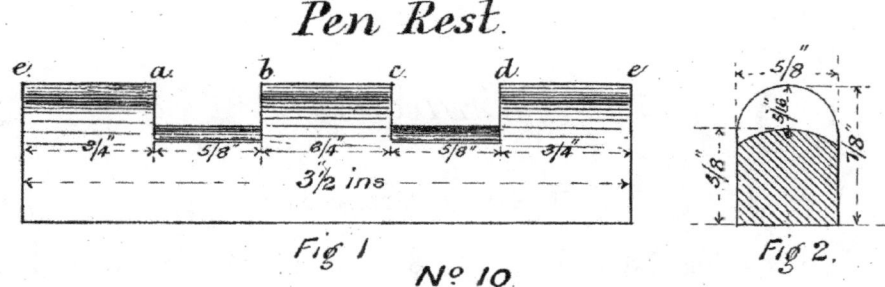

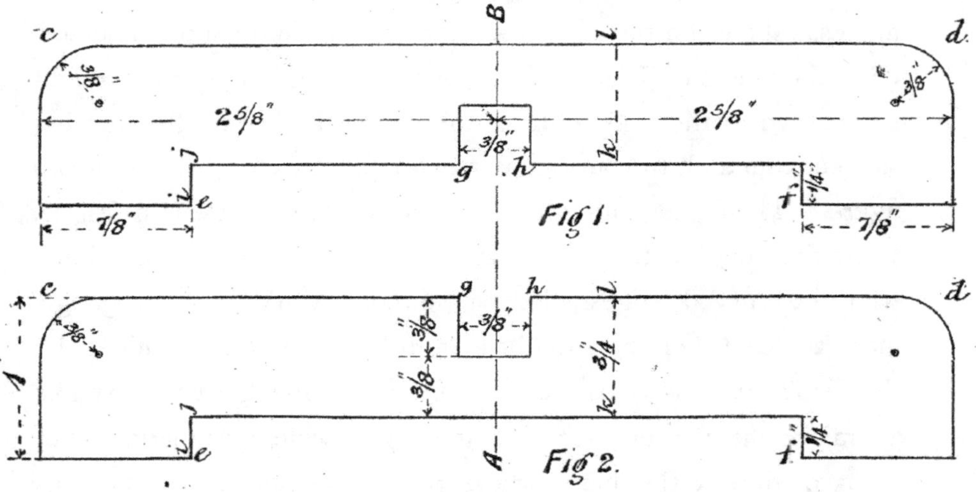

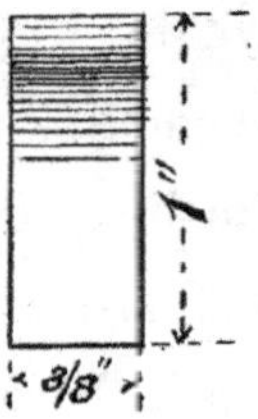

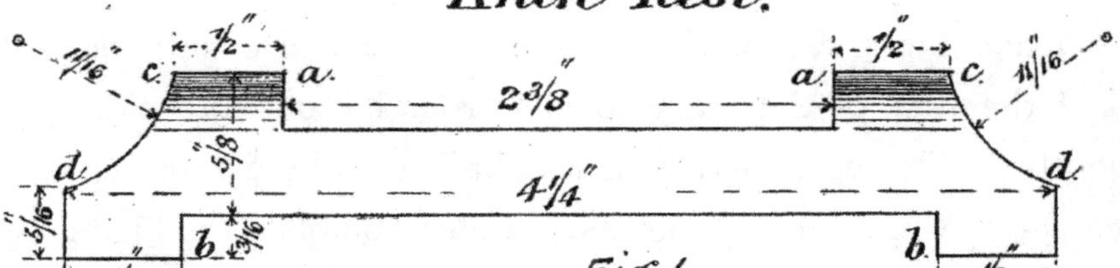

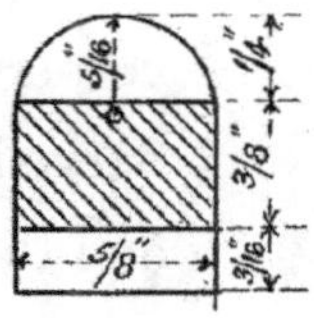

No. 12. Paper-Knife.

(Requiring Exercises 5, 7, 12, 8, 9, 10, 22, 16, 6, 23, 13, and 24.)

Cut from Beech a very straight-grained piece, 14 in. long, 2 in. wide, and $\frac{3}{8}$ in. thick. Plane one side and one edge at right angles. Then, on the planed side, to the size and shape indicated, draw the whole of Fig. 1 of drawings No. 12, letting the straight edge serve as the line from A to B. With the smaller turning saw cut round all the curved parts, carefully adhering to the drawn figure. Then gauge all round for thickness, as shown in Fig. 2, plane the rough side down to the gauge lines, and with the knife trim the curved edges where required. With the set gauge, mark the centre of the straight edge from A to B, and guided by that centre, pare down each corner of the straight edge, so as to make a straight chamfer on each side about $\frac{1}{4}$ in. wide, terminating with a sharp edge at the place where the gauge line was drawn, as shown in Fig. 2. Pare down the corners of both chamfers, and pare each side symmetrically, so as to produce a blade gradually diminishing throughout from a back $\frac{3}{16}$ in. thick to a sharp edge. Then pare down the end of the back to a lancet-shaped point, as shown in Fig. 2. Round the corners of both edges of the handle, so as to make them symmetrical throughout, and also pare the corners of the back of the blade so as to round it on both sides very slightly. File judiciously with a light hand where required, and then, for the first time using the scraper, complete the blade with great care by scraping, finishing as usual with sand-paper.

No. 14. Bowl for Toilette, &c.

(Requiring Exercises 5, 7, 12, 8, 9, 10, 15, 26, 13, 28, 29, 6, and 24.)

This model is shown in the perspective Fig. 1 of drawings No. 14. Commence for it by cutting from Beech a piece about 5 in. long, 3 in. wide, and 1¼ in. thick. Plane one side and one edge at right angles. Then gauge for a thickness of 1 in. and plane the rough side to the gauge lines. Determine by choice which side shall be the bottom of the bowl and which the top. Find the centre of the bottom side by drawing the lines from A to B and from C to D as shown in Fig. 2. Repeat these lines on the edges and top side, using the try square. Then, on the bottom side, with compasses and square, draw the whole of the figures constituting the entire diagram shown by Fig. 2, and on the top side draw freehand the larger oval or ellipse diagram shown by Fig. 3, being guided by the points of the guide-lines first drawn for the purpose.

Then, with the turning saw, cut round by the line of the ellipse on the top side, and finish the edge square with chisel and file. Then, with finger and pencil, mark a line about ⅛ in. inside the outer edge all round the larger ellipse. With a ⅝-in. gouge cut out the centre so as to form the inside of the bowl, the depth and shape being shown by the dotted lines of Fig 4.

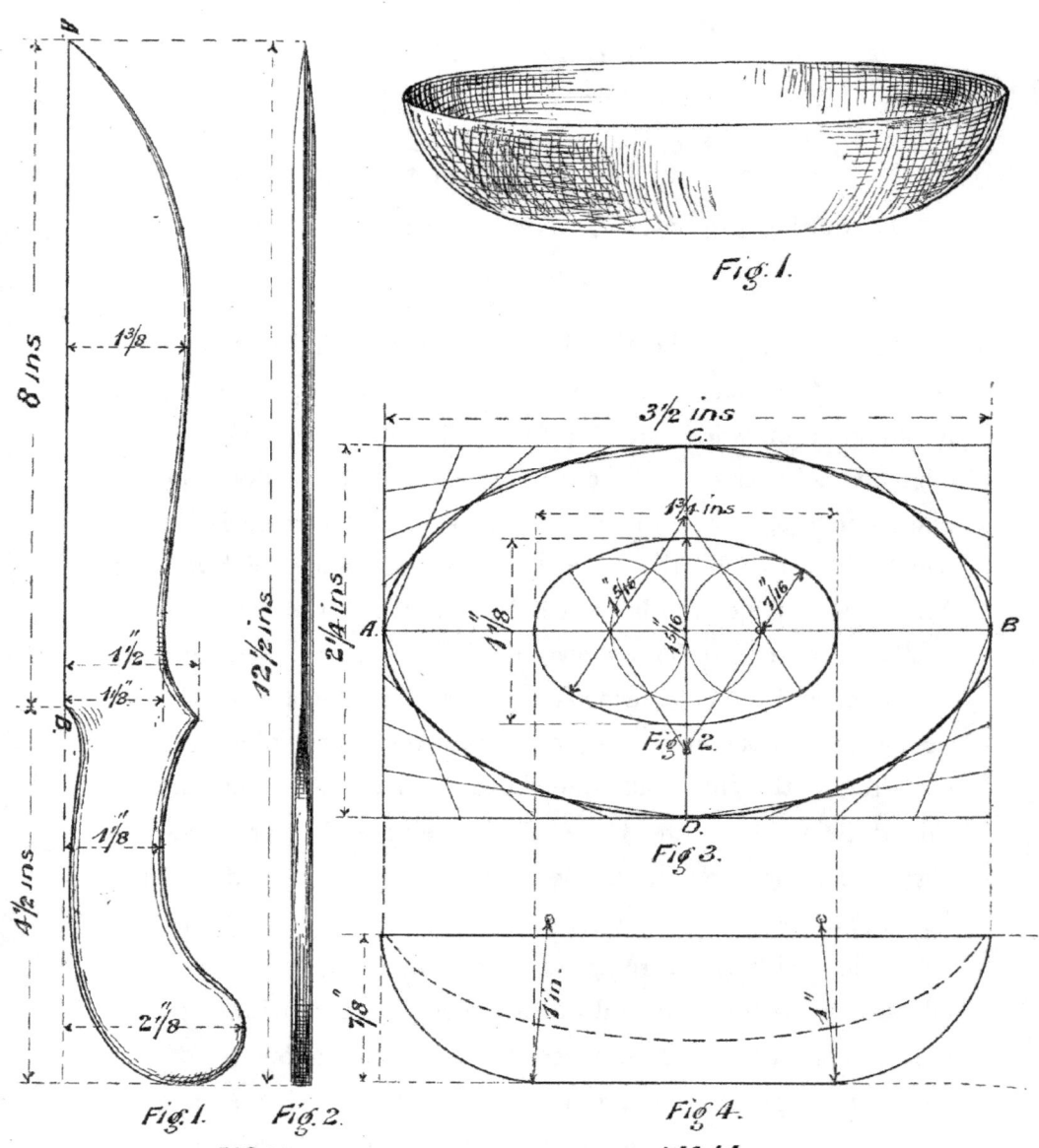

Fig. 1.

Fig. 1. Fig. 2.
Nº 12.
Paper Knife

Fig. 2.
Fig. 3.
Fig 4.
Nº 14.
Bowl for toilette or writing table

Having so symmetrically shaped the inside and made it as smooth as the gouge is capable of, with the round end of the scraper dress as smoothly as possible, and finish with sand-paper, before proceeding with the bottom side.

To complete the bottom side, leave the ellipse in the centre untouched, and from its outline to the outer edge of the lip of the bowl, shave with the knife so as to produce in all directions a curve corresponding to those at each end of Fig. 4. Take a shaving off the flat bottom with the smoothing plane, so as to remove the compass marks. Then file judiciously and lightly where required, scrape perfectly smooth, and finish with sand-paper.

₊ This No. 14 is a very interesting study and a keen test of application, care, and skill, anything like carelessness being sure to leave its tell-tale marks.

No. 15. Hammer-Handle.

(Requiring Exercises 5, 7, 12, 8, 9, 22, 30, 4, 31, 2, 13, and 24.)

This study exercises ability in the mastery of elliptical lines, and in the use of the spokeshave in Exercises 30 and 31.

Cut from Beech a piece about 13 in. long, 1½ in. wide, and 1¼ in. thick. Plane one side and one edge at right angles. On the smooth side thus produced, with the pencil sketch throughout the whole of Fig. 1 of drawings No. 15. Then, with the turning saw, cut at right angles to the curved lines on both edges throughout, and finish the shaping with the spokeshave, taking care to maintain right angles. Then, on one of the edges, with pencil, sketch throughout the whole of Fig. 2, and, with saw and spokeshave, shape both sides in unison with that sketch, still carefully maintaining right angles throughout. Then, with the knife, shave off the corners so as so make four symmetrical chamfers throughout. Then, with the spokeshave, remove the corners of the chamfers, and proceed with the paring down until the required symmetrical elliptical shape is arrived at, as shown by Figs. 1, 2, and 3. Saw across at right angles at each end to the exact length, and finish with file, scraper, and sand-paper.

No. 16. Handle for Chisel or File.

(Requiring Exercises 5, 7, 8, 9, 10, 11, 33, 18, 6, 2, 13, and 24.)

From Beech cut a piece 6 in. long, 2 in. wide, and 1¼ in. thick. Plane one side and one edge at right angles. Gauge for greatest width shown from *A* to *B* in Fig. 1 of drawings No. 16, and also for greatest thickness shown by *A* to *B* in Fig. 2. Plane the rough side and edge down to the respective gauge lines, thus producing a piece of equal thickness throughout, with the sides and edges at right angles. Saw across one end at right angles. On the face thus produced on that end sketch Fig. 3 complete.

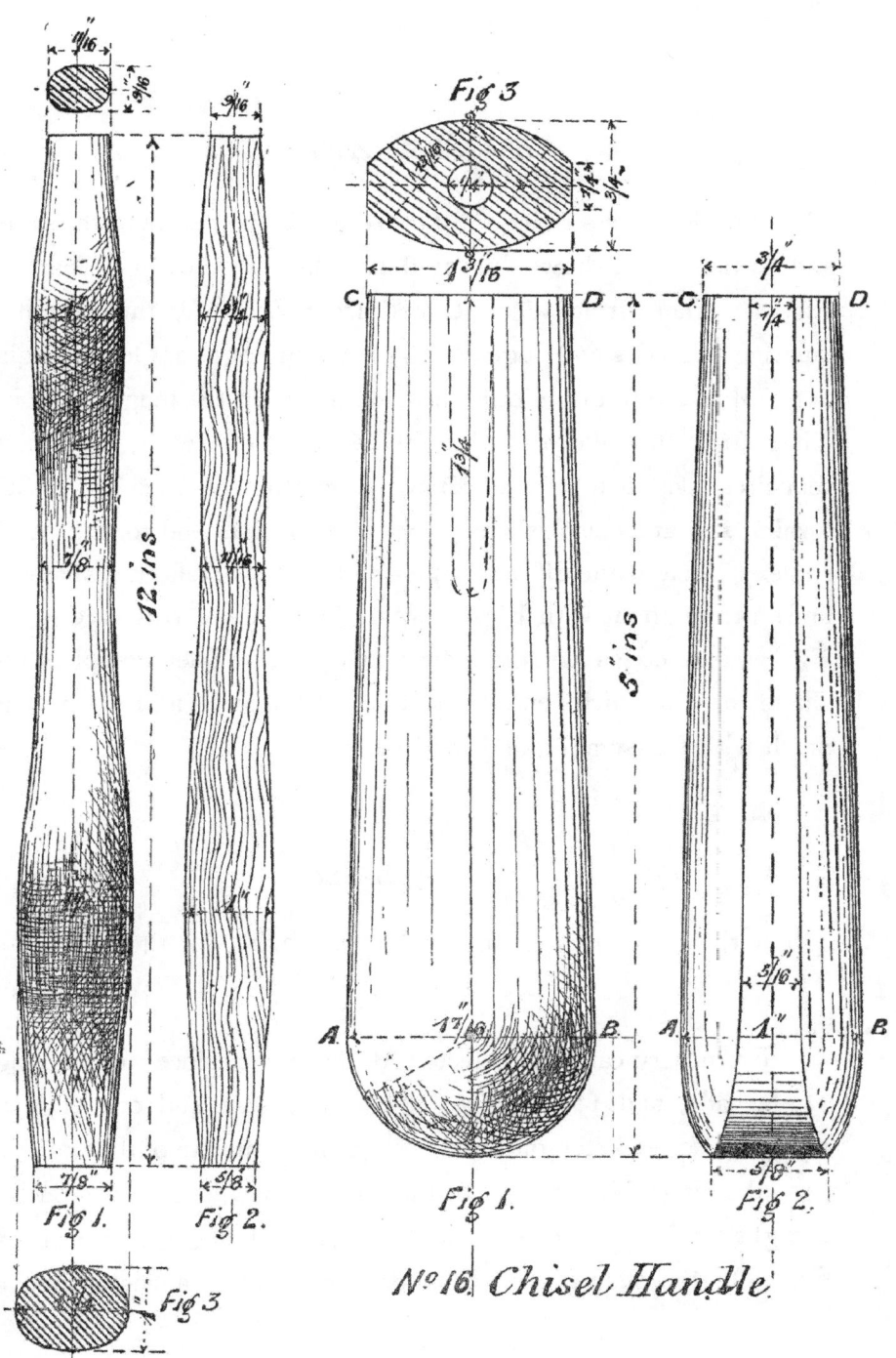

N°15. Hammer Handle

N°16. Chisel Handle

Fit a ¼-in. Bit to the Brace and bore a hole in the centre of the same end to the depth shown by the dotted lines in the upper part of Fig. 1. Plane from A to C and from B to D, thus slightly tapering the sides and edges, but maintaining right angles throughout. Measure from the thin flat end and mark the length of 5 in. Then, from the centre of the line A to B of Fig. 1, describe a semicircle on each side as shown at bottom of Fig. 1. With turning saw and chisel, shape each side of that end to the semicircle. Then plane off the angles so far as to make the shape in unison throughout with Fig. 3, presenting sides corresponding to Fig. 1, and edges corresponding to Fig. 2. Then complete the shape of the thick end with knife, as shown in Fig. 2, and finish with file, scraper, and sand-paper.

No. 17. Spoon.

(Requiring Exercises 5, 19, 12, 8, 9, 10, 32, 22, 29, 14, 15, 26, 13, 2, 8, 6, 24, 16, and 1.)

From very carefully selected Beech cut a piece 10 in. long, 2½ in. wide, and 1¾ in. thick. Plane one side and one edge at right angles. Sketch on the flat edge the complete outline of Fig. 1 of drawings No. 17. With the turning saw, cut to the outline at right angles on the upper side only, completing with chisel and file. On the shaped side thus produced, make a centre line as shown in Fig. 2, then the cross lines. Then, with compasses as guides and checks, mark the outlines of the handle shown in Fig. 2, and, with freehand, sketch the ellipse. With bits and brace drill a ⅞-in. hole right through at each centre marked b, and a ⅜-in. hole at each centre marked c. Then, with the turning saw, cut to the outline at right angles throughout, completing the process with gouge, knife, and file. Then, in the manner described for making the inside of No. 14, make the inside of the Spoon in unison with the dotted curve of Fig. 1.

The inside of the Spoon being thus completed, proceed with the outside. Mark on the edge the outline $d\,d\,d\,d\,d$ for the under side of the spoon. With the turning saw, cut out to that outline, and round with the knife, as shown in the sections of Figs. 3, 4, and 5. Take care to keep carefully outside the lines when cutting with the knife, and apply the file, scraper, and sand-paper for finishing.

₊ The under part of the spoon is a capital exercise in modelling with the knife, and, if one process is completed before the next is commenced, requires no more than ordinary application and care.

No. 18. Chopping-Board.

(Requiring Exercises 5, 12, 8, 9, 10, 14, 15, 26, 34, 13, 25, and 24.)

This especially involves straight and square planing. Cut from Deal a piece 20 in. long, 6½ in. wide, and 1 in. thick. Plane

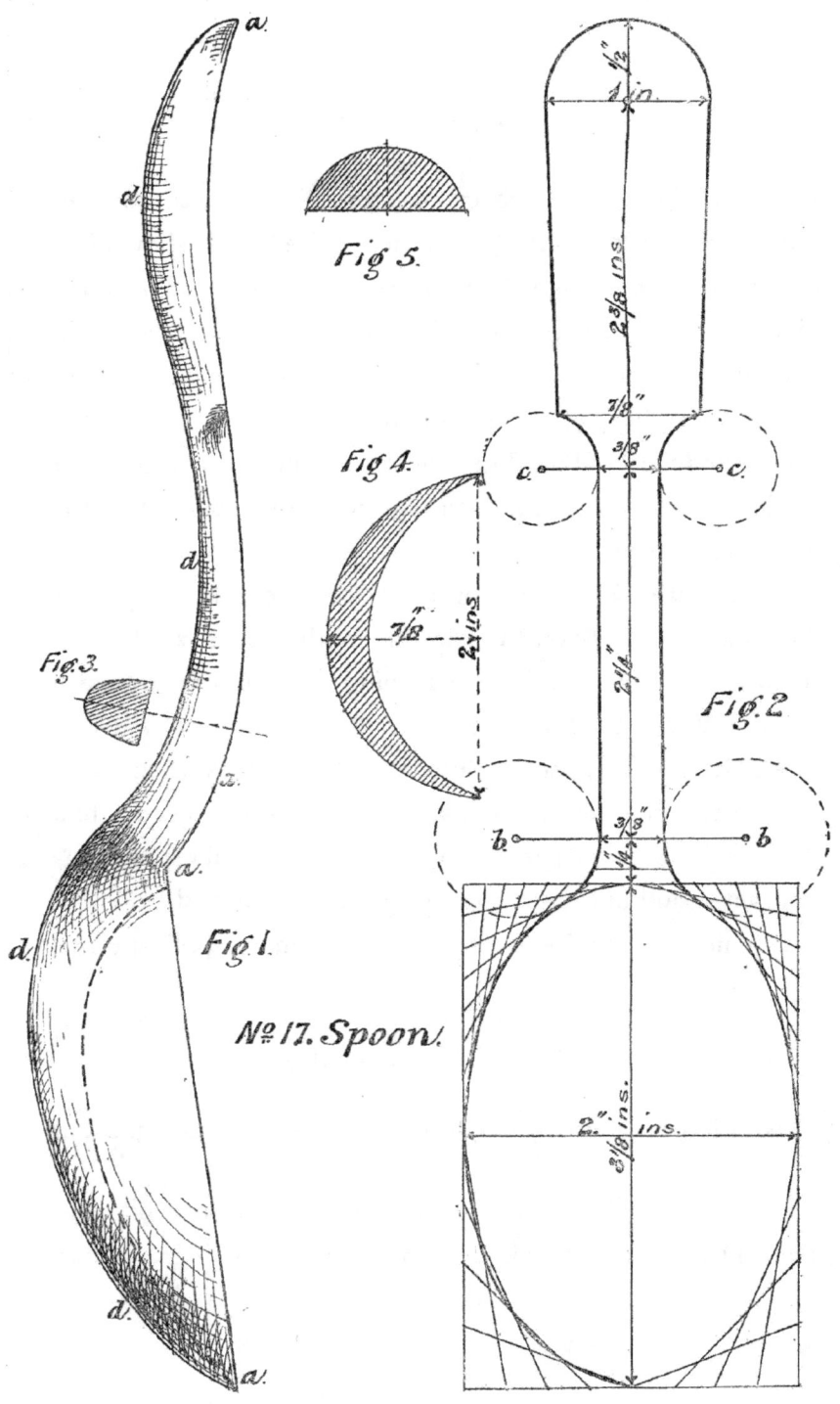

one side perfectly level and one edge perfectly straight at right angles. Gauge and mark for width at 5¾ in. Find and mark the centre line A to B in Fig. 1 of drawings No. 18. Set the compasses to a radius from A to B, and describe, with A for the centre, the semicircle shown at the top of the Fig. Fit a 1-in. Centre-bit to the Brace, and drill a hole with A for the centre, taking care that it goes vertically through at right angles, and that there is no splitting when the bit is nearly through. With the small turning saw, cut round the semicircle at right angles, and, with the chisel, shave off and round the two corners that spring from the semicircle, also at right angles. Then, measuring from the centre of the rounded end at B, mark the entire length at 16⅞ in., and, with the tenon saw, cut off at the mark at right angles. Then shave and round at right angles the two bottom corners. Plane the bottom edge smooth, and file the edges where necessary. Set the gauge at ¾ in., mark with it the edge all round for thickness, and plane the rough side down to the mark, perfectly level throughout. Then, with the smoothing plane, take a thin shaving from the first side, merely enough to remove the marks, taking care to maintain an accurate level. Finish throughout with sandpaper.

*** The object of deferring the planing of the second side until so late a period, is that, at the same time, minute chipping and roughness of edge on that side, almost certain to result from the boring and sawing, are at the same time disposed of.

No. 19. Half-Yard Measure.

(In the original Sloyd model this is a half-metre measure.)

(Requiring Exercises 5, 7, 12, 8. 9, 10, 25, 30, 15, 16, 6, 2, 13, and 24.)

Select from Beech an exceptionally straight-grained piece 24 in. long, 1¼ in. wide, and ¾ in. thick. Plane one side and one edge at right angles, both scrupulously straight and even; then gauge, mark to a nicety for 1⅛ in. wide and ½ in. thick, and plane to the gauge marks with great exactitude, thus producing a four-cornered rod of uniform size throughout. Saw across one end at right angles. Measure from that cut end, mark the length of 18 in., and saw across at the mark. Then set the gauge precisely at ⅞ in., and, passing it along each edge, mark on both sides for the lines *a* to *b* in Fig. 1 of drawings No 19, continuing the lines from end to end of the entire rod. Then, with the square, mark across the place for *a a*, and there saw a slit on each side down to the gauge line. Then proceed to the first exercise in Obstacle Planing (No. 25.) Thus, pass the smooth plane along each edge from *b* to *a*, as far as the obstacle of the corner will allow. Of course the planing cannot be continued into the corners, but, whatever is left by the plane must be got out by the chisel and file. Then, on each side, sketch for the handle, as shown in Fig. 1, the gauge line, previously there, forming part of the sketch. Then, with the turning-saw, cut out

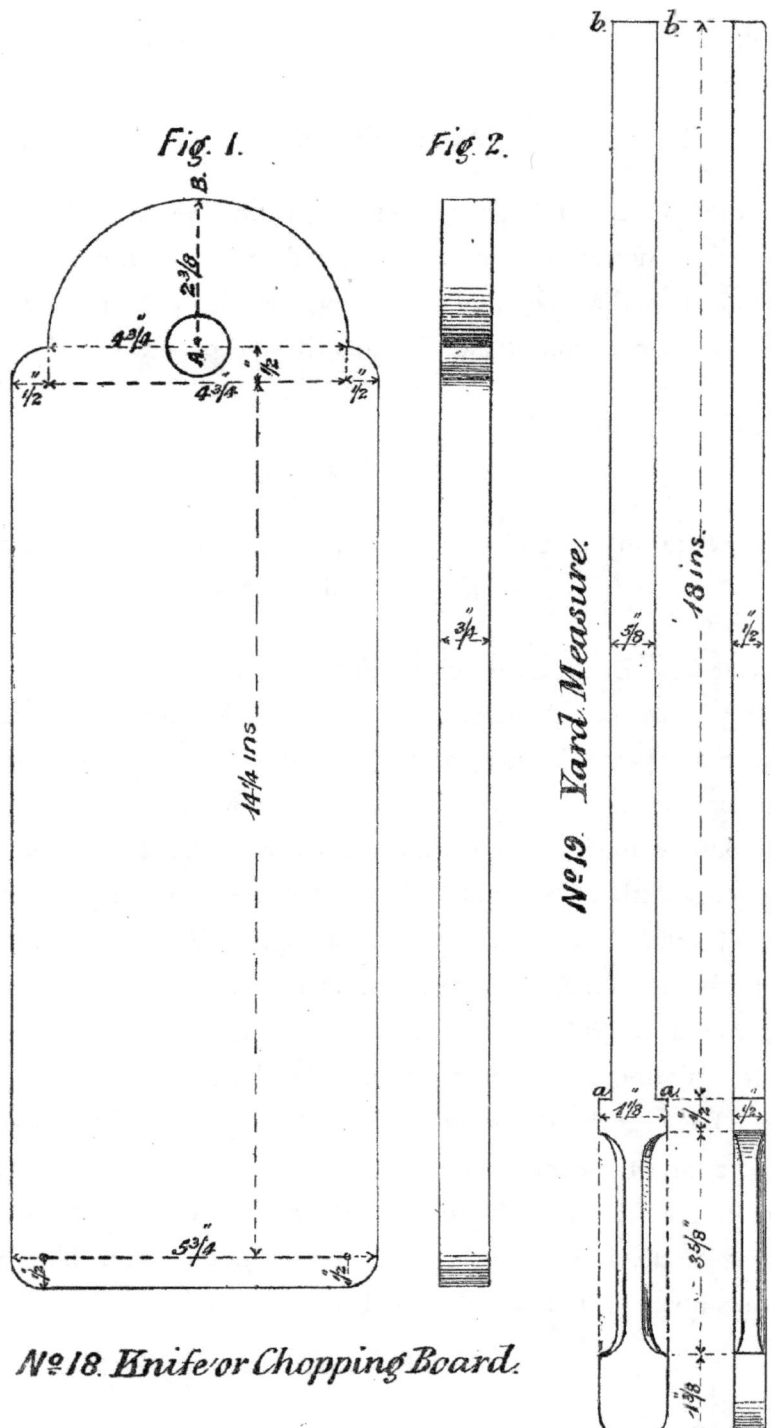

to the sketch and gauge lines. With the knife, make the chamfers shown in Figs. 1 and 2. Then shave the corners and round the end of the handle, as shown in Fig. 1. File and scrape lightly where required, and finish with sand-paper.

No. 20. Scoop.

(Requiring Exercises 5, 19, 12, 9, 14, 7, 15, 26, 32, 33, 29, 28, 13, 18, 6, 16, 2, and 24.)

Cut from Beech a carefully-selected piece 11 in. long, 3 in. wide, and 3 in. thick. Plane one side and one edge at right angles, with exceptional care. Then, on the smooth edge sketch the outline of the upper side *a* to *a* of Fig. 1 of drawings No. 20. Saw to the outline at right angles throughout, afterwards correcting inaccuracies with chisel and plane. On the smooth shaped side thus produced, sketch the outline of Fig. 2. With $1\frac{1}{2}$-in. centre bit drill the holes indicated by *b b*, right through. Saw to the outline all round, carefully maintaining right angles throughout and, as before, correcting inaccuracies with chisel and plane.

Then, at the upper edge of the invisible end at the bottom of Fig. 2, find the centre represented by *c* in Fig. 3. Fix compasses to a radius from *c* to *d*, and, from the centre before found, describe a semicircle, and from the same centre another semicircle with a radius about $\frac{1}{8}$ in. longer. The centre of the inner of those semicircles represents the bottom of the inside of the Scoop at f of Fig. 1, and the outer one represents the bottom of the outside at the same point.

Next, with ⅛-in. gouge, make a furrow just inside the outline of the face of the scoop, as previously recommended for Model No. 17. Then, from that furrow as a starting-point, in all directions, with ⅜-gouge, scoop out from back to front, to the depth indicated by the dotted line of Fig. 1, and to the width at front of the semicircle previously drawn on the end, but gradually diminishing the inner capacity so as to make it smallest near the handle, in about the same proportion as indicated for the bottom by the dotted line in Fig. 1. Then file and scrape inside where required, and finish so far with sand-paper.

Then, upon each edge, draw the outline of the bottom of the Scoop, shown in Fig. 1. Saw throughout that outline at right angles. Then from e to f plane all round to the semicircle indicated by the outer line of Fig. 3 previously described on the end. Then, with the knife, cut the handle to the section indicated by Fig. 4, and continue the shaping to e as indicated by the shaded lines of Fig. 1. File the handle and outside of Scoop where required, and finish with sand-paper.

⁎ The most difficult part of this model is that shaded in Fig. 1, which requires special attention and care.

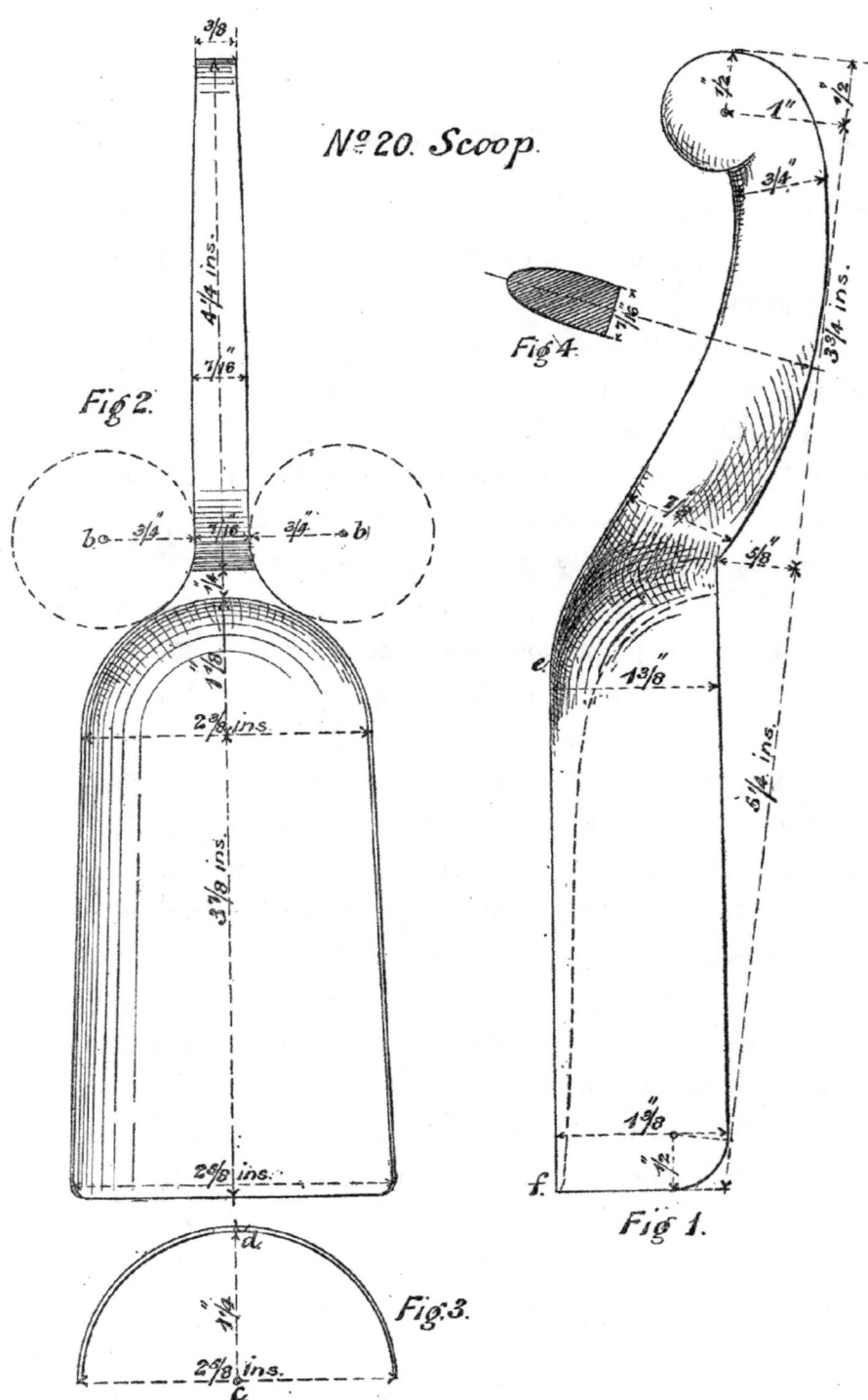

No. 21. Hanging Pegs or Rack.

(Requiring Exercises 5, 7, 12, 8, 9, 10, 14, 15, 26, 13, 18, 4, 26, 37, 29, 35, 39, 40, and 42.)

From Deal cut out two pieces, one 18 in. long, $3\frac{1}{2}$ in. wide, and $\frac{7}{8}$ in. thick; the other 15 in. long, 1 in. wide, and $\frac{7}{8}$ in. thick.

Commencing with the larger piece, plane one side and one edge at right angles. Then gauge-mark to a width of 3 in., and plane the rough edge down to that mark. At the centre of the width draw a line from end, as shown in Fig. 1, f to f. On that line, with compasses, mark the points indicated by a, b, c, of Fig. 1 of the drawings No. 21. At each point drill a $\frac{5}{8}$-in. hole right through, taking great care to drill vertically. With the square, draw the cross lines at $d\ d$, the intersections with the central line forming additional central points. Set compasses to a radius of $\frac{7}{8}$ in., and, from each of those central points, describe a semicircle as shown in the Fig.; then from each of the same central points describe an outer semicircle as also shown in the Fig. With tenon saw make a nick at each of the four points g, in each case reaching to the outer of the semicircles, each nick being strictly at right angles. Then, with turning saw, follow the line of each of the outer semicircles. Then dress the edges all round with chisel and file as required. Then gauge-mark all round for a thickness of $\frac{3}{4}$ in., and plane the rough side down to the mark, evenly throughout. Gauge-mark all round for the chamfer, in the proportion shown in Fig. 1, and chamfer to the mark accordingly, using the plane for the sides and the knife for the curves and corners. File throughout where necessary, and finish with sandpaper.

The smaller piece of Deal being to make the pegs with, plane it on one side and one edge at right angles, then gauge-mark for a width of ¾ in. and for a thickness of ⅜ in., as illustrated in section by Fig. 4. Saw across into three lengths of 5 in. each. Place them together on their sides, and sketch one side of each as shown from j to k and l in Fig. 3, leaving the space from j to m untouched. With the try square repeat the lines of this sketch on both sides of each. With saw and knife cut each peg to the sketch, finishing the whole, excepting the circular plug. Then at the inner end, find the centre as denoted in Fig. 4, and, using the same centre-bit as for Fig. 1, describe a circle mark as dotted in Fig. 4. Then, with the tenon saw, cut by the "shoulder" to a depth of ⅛ in., and pare the circle with the knife to the shoulder j, so making a round plug, a little too large to go into the holes of Fig. 1. Then, with the file, carefully reduce the size of each plug so as to very accurately and tightly fit one hole at a time in Fig 1, where wedging must not be tolerated. The perfection of this part of the work is to be tested by ascertaining that the pegs are precisely in a line, and that each one fits all round to the face of the board into which it is inserted.

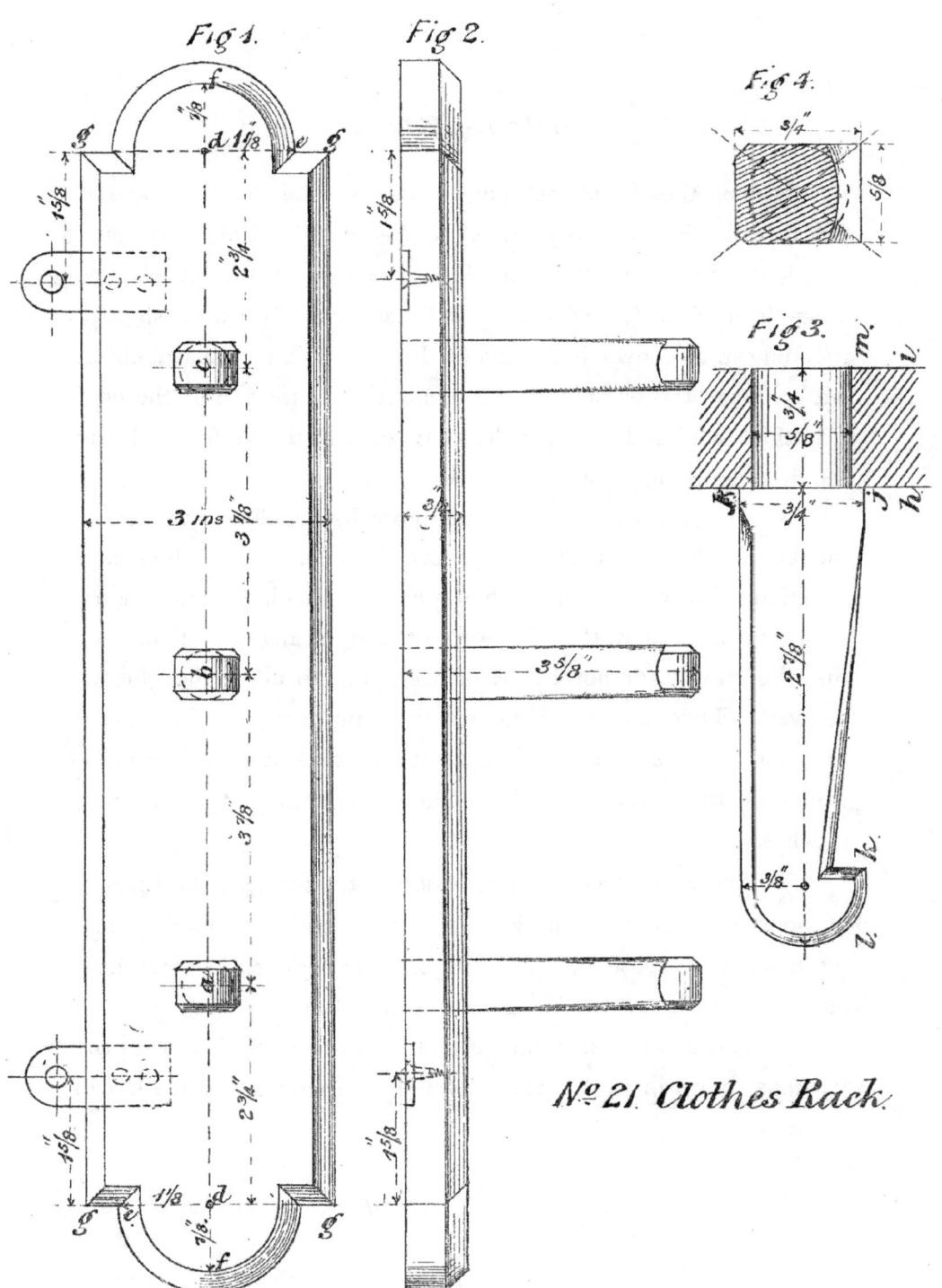

No. 21. Clothes Rack.

Having thus fitted each plug to its own hole, and marked it for identification, the pegs may be completed. Cut down each one, with the tenon saw, from k to x, and, with the chisel, pare down from j to k, first making it square and afterwards slightly rounding it, as shown in section of Fig. 4. With a sharp chisel cut round to the outside of the semicircle for the top of the peg. File this round and then cut the chamfer with the knife. File as required, and finish with sand-paper.

The pegs being thus made ready for fixing, clean the face of the board (Fig. 1) with the smooth plane, and the edges and chamfers with sand-paper. Then glue in each plug, using the try square to make sure that they project at right angles. Then put the whole away for not less than six hours, to allow the glue to set well. Then, as each plug has been purposely made slightly too long, saw off each projection at the back, and smooth the whole of the back with the plane, so effecting the finishing touches.

To avoid the necessity for nailing to the wall, get two pieces of hoop-iron about $1\frac{1}{2}$ in. long and $\frac{1}{2}$ in. wide. To adapt each piece for its purpose, cut one end round and punch in a nail-hole and two smaller screw holes, as shown in Fig. 1. With a chisel cut a neat recess for each iron so that it can be sunk flush with the back, as shown in Fig. 2, and, inserting the screws, the work will be complete.

No. 22. Flower-Pot Stand.

(Requiring Exercises 5, 7, 12, 8, 9, 10, 34, 20, 2, 1, 13, 41, 42, and 35.)

This is an especially good subject for straight sawing, straight planing, and nailing.

Cut from Deal a piece about 22 in. long, 6 in. wide, and 1 in. thick. With the jack-plane face one side and one edge perfectly straight and true at right angles. Gauge-mark for $1\frac{3}{8}$ in. thick, and plane the rough side down to the gauge-line. Square one end with the plane, mark to length shown in Fig. 1 of drawings No. 22, cut with tenon saw to mark, and square the end with smooth plane. Then gauge-mark for thickness of lath shown in Fig. 4, and saw off a shade inside the guage-lines. In like manner cut five laths, and plane each to the gauge line.

The laths being thus made, sufficient wood will be left for the supports. Make the width of the supports the same as that of the laths. After gauging and planing the supports to depth as Fig. 4, saw off to the 6-in. length. Square the ends with a chisel and set out on each the distance *a a*, Fig. 3. Gauge to *b b*, Fig. 4, and with the tenon saw, cut to the gauge-line at *a a*, and with the knife remove the piece between *a* and *a*. Then mark on each lath the distance the supports are from each end of the laths, and nail on the laths—the outside laths first, then the centre one, and finally the other two.

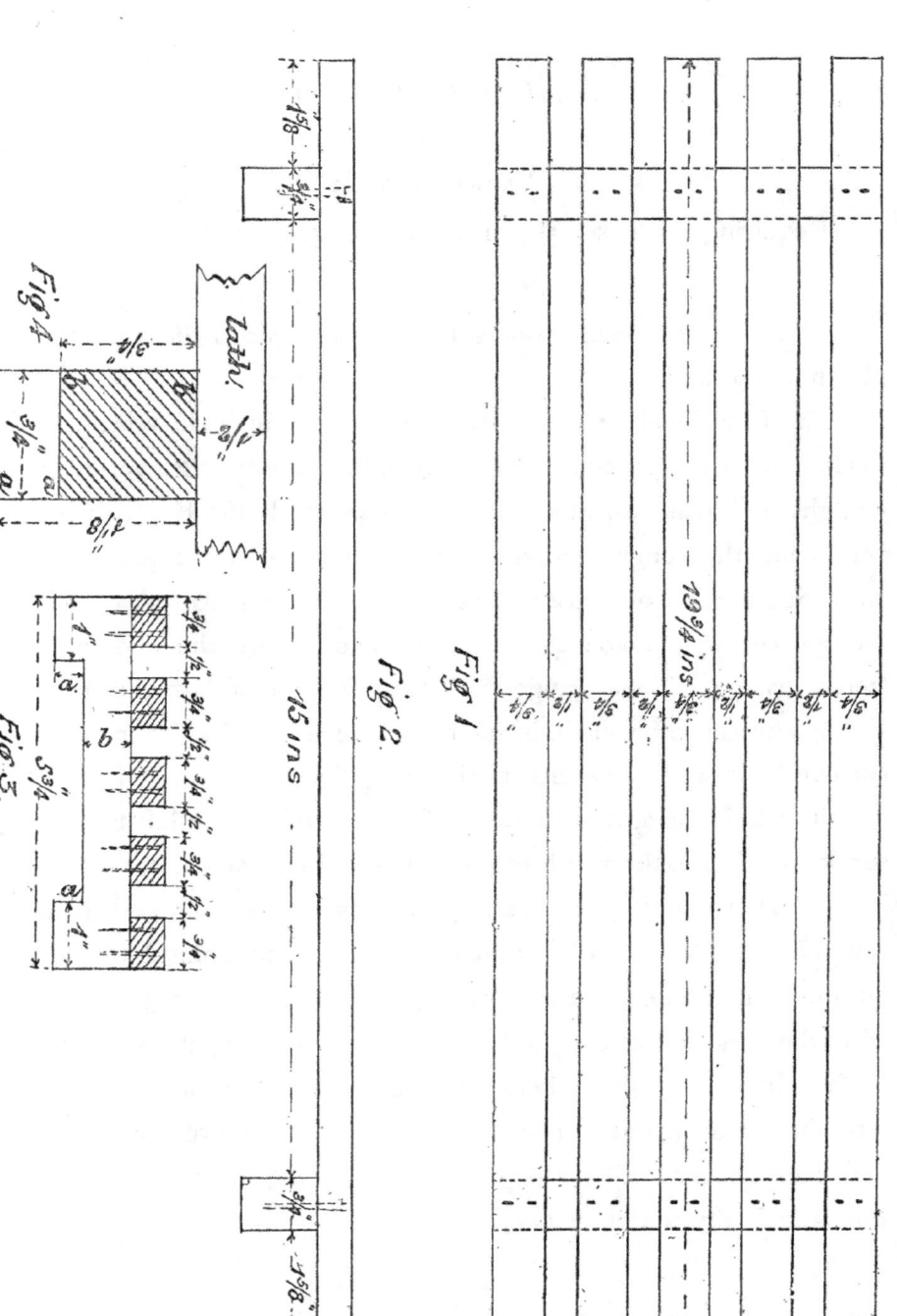

No. 23. Foot-Stool.

(Requiring Exercises 5, 7, 12, 8, 9, 10, 3, 4, 15, 44, 32, 29, 14, 13, 3, 5, 41, and 42.)

Cut from Deal two pieces, one 12 in. long, 6 in. wide, and 1¼ in. thick; the other 18 in. long, 3¼ in. wide, and 1 in. thick.

The former piece is for the laths, and it must be prepared and cut as in No. 22, making each lath to finish 1 in. wide, ½ in. thick, and 10¾ in. long.

The wood for the support must now be proceeded with. Plane one side and one edge at right angles, and gauge-mark for width of 3 in. and thickness of 1⅞ in. Plane the rough side and edge down to the gauge-marks. Then saw through the centre so as to make two pieces of ⅞ in. thickness each. Place the pieces side by side, and nail them together with two 1½-in. wrought nails, so that both pieces can be operated upon together. Then draw on one outer side the diagram shown on the unshaded part of Fig. 1 of drawings No. 23, and, with the aid of try-square and compasses, repeat the diagram on the other outer side. Then cut off each end nearly to the end lines of the diagrams, and, with the smoothing plane, finish at perfect right angles. Then, with a ⅝-in. centre-bit, drill at the spots marked *a a* on each diagram, penetrating on one side a little more than an inch, and finishing by drilling from the other side in precise unison. The drilling throughout must be exactly vertical. Then proceed with the arch shown in Fig. 1, With the turning saw cutting out the three semicircles, which finish with gouge and file, taking care to maintain right angles at every point. Then separate the pieces, smooth each face with the smoothing plane, and the circular parts with file and sand-paper.

The respective parts being now complete, mark on each lath the distance the supports are from the ends shown in Fig. 2. Then nail on the laths, *b b* first, *c* next, and the others afterwards. Then, having first taken care to punch down all the nails sufficiently, plane a few shavings off the tops of the laths to make them clean and level.

⁎ If the laths are well and truly nailed on, their ends should be in perfect line. Any defect in that respect must be remedied by carefully and judiciously planing; but the perfection of work is when no such planing is necessary.

No. 24. Book-Carrier.

(Requiring Exercises 5, 12, 8, 9, 10, 3, 4, 15, 44, 32, 29, 14, 13, 3, 5, 41, and 42.)

This is made partly in hard and partly in soft wood.

For the handle, cut from Beech a piece 8 in. long, 2 in. wide, and $\frac{7}{8}$ in. thick. Plane one side and one edge. Then gauge-mark for $1\frac{1}{2}$ in. wide and $\frac{3}{4}$ in. thick, and plane the rough side and edge down to each gauge-mark. Then draw on one side the diagram of the handle shown in Fig. 1 of drawings No. 24. With

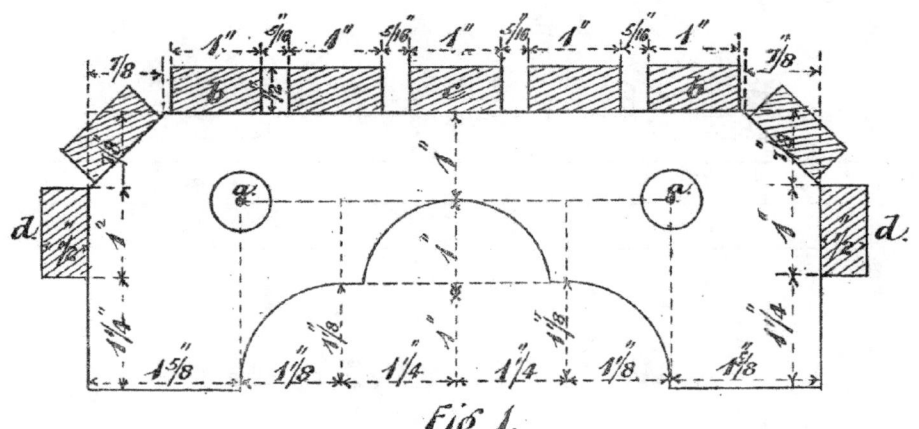

No. 23. Foot Stool.

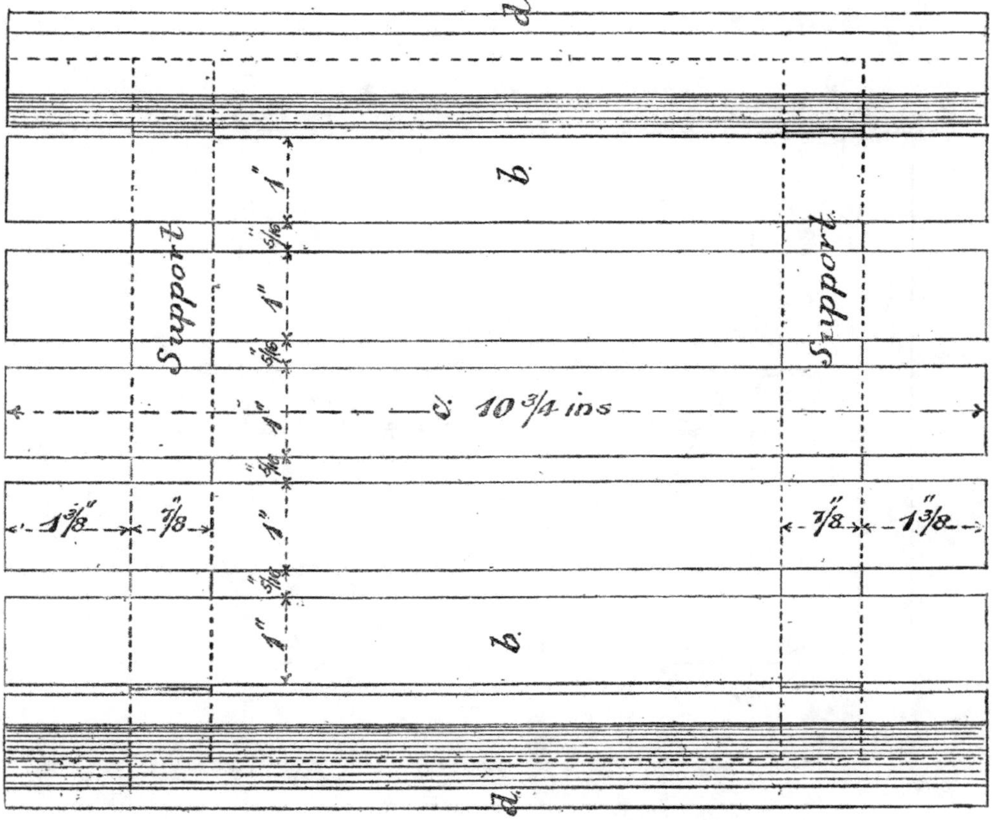

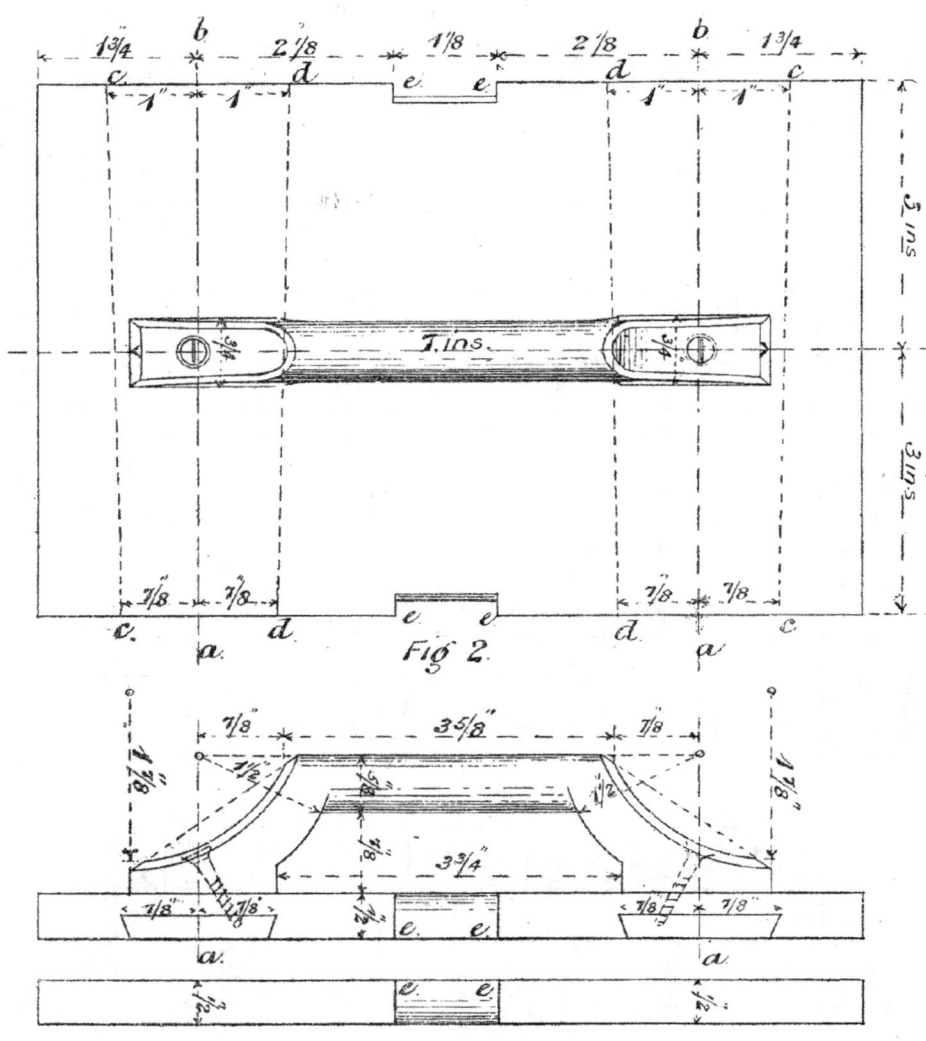

Fig 2.

Fig 4.

No 24 Book Carrier

the turning saw, cut to the inner and outer lines of the diagram. With the plane, round the top of the handle, as shown in Fig. 1, and, with the knife, round and smooth the other parts, taking care that all the right angles are strictly maintained. Then, with an $\frac{1}{8}$-in. centre-bit, drill a hole for each screw, as shown in the Fig., and, with the knife, counter-sink for the heads of the screws. With the knife, make the chamfers at the corners of the curves, as shown in Fig. 2, and finish completely with scraper and sand-paper.

The handle being thus finished, cut from Deal a piece 24 in. long, $6\frac{1}{2}$ in. wide, and $\frac{5}{8}$ in. thick, and plane one side and one edge at right angles. Gauge-mark for 6 in. wide, and $\frac{1}{2}$ in. thick, and plane the rough side and edge down to the gauge-marks. Square one end, measuring from that end, saw off at 9 in. On the larger piece remaining, draw the lines *a b* and *a b* in the positions shown in Fig. 2 ; then, with the compasses, set off the spaces from *a* to *c* and from *a* to *c*, *b* to *c* and *b* to *c*, *a* to *d* and *a* to *d*, *b* to *d* and *b* to *d*. Then set the gauge to half the thickness, and with it mark the edges on the four places indicated in each case from *c* to *d*. Set the bevel to the oblique line at each side of the dovetails, and transfer this bevelled line to each side at points *c c c c* and *d d d d* Then, with tenon saw, cut down each line *c d* to the depth of the gauge line, and, with a small chisel, remove the whole of the pieces between the nicks made by the saw. This will result in two grooves for dovetailed tongues, as shown above, *a a* in Fig. 1, designed to strengthen and prevent from warping the upper half of the holder.

The grooves having been thus made ready, the dovetails must be prepared. From Deal cut two pieces, each 9 in. long, 2½ in. wide, and ¾ in. thick. Plane one side of each and bevel one edge to the pitch the bevel was previously set for. Then, on the planed side, mark 2¼ in. at one end, 1¼ in. at the other end, and take to that width, afterwards bevelling the edge as before. Then fit each of the tongues provided, driving them tight into their places. When they fit exactly, glue the planed side and the edges, and drive them to their positions, being careful not to split off the ends. Then allow time for the glue to set, and cut off the projecting ends of the tongues and plane them and the face of the board to a level. Cut off to exact length, measuring from the lines *a b*. Then smooth both boards with the plane, nail them together with two small nails, and square the ends. Then gauge and nick with the saw for the recesses *e e*, removing the wood from each recess with the knife, so making grooves for a strap to pass round. Then screw on the handle in the manner indicated by both Figs., and finish as required with sand-paper.

No. 25. Ladle.
(Requiring Exercises 5, 19, 12, 9, 10, 32, 15, 33, 29, 14, 26, 28, 22, 49, 31, 1, 6, 16, 13, and 24.)

Cut from Beech a piece 16 in. long, 4 in. wide, and 4 in. thick. The manner of proceeding resembles that required for No. 17. Plane one side and one edge at right angles, and draw on the planed

Nº 25. Ladle.

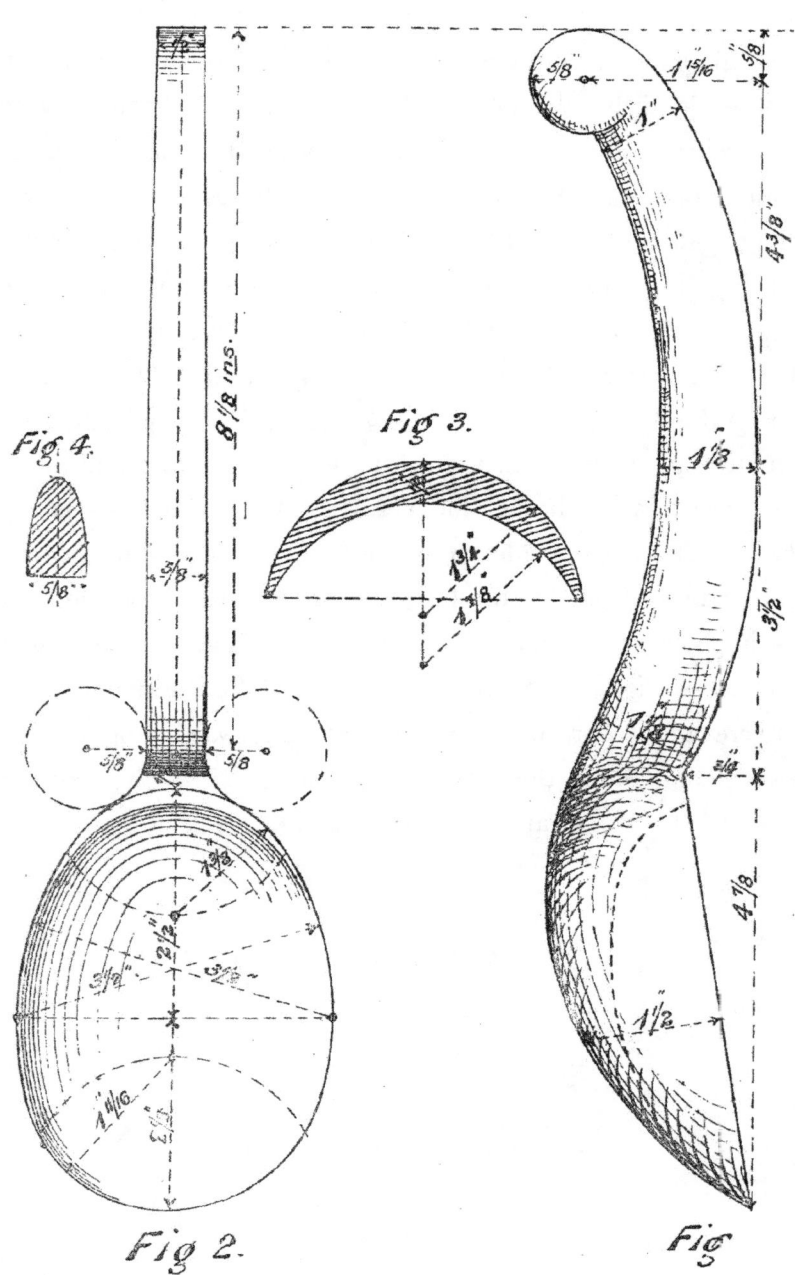

side the diagram shown in Fig. 2 of drawings No. 25. With a 1¼-in. centre-bit, drill two holes right through, as indicated by the dotted circles. Saw round the outside lines of the diagram, taking care not to obliterate the lines. Trim exactly to the lines with a chisel, gouge, and file. Then mark on each edge the upper curved line of Fig. 1. Saw to that line without obliterating it, finishing with spokeshave, plane, chisel, and file. Then cut out the bowl of the ladle, using a small gouge for the edge, and a larger one for obtaining the depth, which must be governed by the white section shown in Fig. 3, and finished with file, scraper, and sand-paper before proceeding with the under side. When the bowl is thus finished, mark on each side the curve for the under side shown in Fig. 1. Saw just outside the line, and proceed to shape the under side—the bowl to the shaded section of Fig. 3, and the handle to the section of Fig. 4. For finishing the bowl, fix the handle in the bench screw, and pare with a wide chisel, afterwards applying the knife for completing the bowl and handle. For the finishing touches use the file, scraper, and sand-paper.

END.

CLASS OF BOYS AT WORK

Elementary Sloyd

AND

Whittling

With Drawings and Working Directions

BY

Gustaf Larsson

Principal of the Sloyd Training School, Boston, Massachusetts

SILVER, BURDETT AND COMPANY
NEW YORK   BOSTON   CHICAGO

Copyright, 1906, by
SILVER, BURDETT AND COMPANY

CONTENTS

	PAGE
INTRODUCTION	1
WOODS OR TIMBER	5
TOOLS AND IMPLEMENTS FOR ELEMENTARY SLOYD (ILLUSTRATED)	12
LIST OF TOOLS AND MATERIALS	17
WORKING DIRECTIONS FOR ELEMENTARY SLOYD (ILLUSTRATED)	37
STAINING AND POLISHING	65
WHITTLING	69
GENERAL DIRECTIONS	70
WORKING DIRECTIONS FOR WHITTLING (ILLUSTRATED)	72
OUTFIT OF TOOLS AND MATERIALS (ILLUSTRATED)	93
SPONTANEOUS CREATIONS BY CHILDREN UNDER TWELVE YEARS OF AGE (ILLUSTRATED)	96

INTRODUCTION

SLOYD is tool work so arranged and employed as to stimulate and promote vigorous, intelligent self-activity for a purpose which the worker recognizes as good. By "Elementary Sloyd" is meant bench work in wood, in two dimensions adapted to children from eight to twelve years of age. In 1889 I published a series of working drawings for "Preliminary Sloyd" with a teachers' "Sloyd Manual of Working Directions." The changes and improvements made since that time are the results gained from the experience of many teachers, and are embodied in the course here outlined.

It is thought by some that children under twelve years of age have not the requisite strength and maturity to handle ordinary wood-working tools, but, owing to the recognized necessity of providing for the vigorous muscular activity of younger children, this course is suggested.

I have endeavored to select larger objects than those commonly given children at this age, so that they may obtain more physical exercise, and, although a good finish should be insisted upon, less accuracy is required. The objects are chosen with special reference to the interests of a child at this age, and are different from those which have been suggested for the three upper grammar grades. This course may include toys and games which appeal to young children.

Many of the objects in this course have been evolved after a careful study of a large variety of children's original work in wood.

Whether we should always allow children to select what they may choose to make, or whether some consideration of logical sequence or graded effort should underlie the work, can best be decided by visiting schools and carefully observing classes engaged in actual work under

INTRODUCTION

different conditions. The point is, I believe, that we should find out whether or not what the child would *like* to do harmonizes with the educational idea of what he had *best* do. For myself, I believe fully in the value of spontaneity in educational work. I also believe that spontaneity may be guided, greatly to the advantage of the child.

The many different kinds of handiwork now experimented with in the lower grades of our public schools are, without doubt, of much value when given by a teacher thoroughly competent and interested in his work, and they also have the advantage of being taught in the regular schoolroom, by the regular grade teacher, and with inexpensive outfit. Such work, however, can never take the place of sloyd, which, with its large variety of tools and exercises, provides for more free and vigorous muscular movements and offers a more stimulating motive to the worker in the objects which he makes.

"Elementary Sloyd" is suggested for use in the fifth and sixth grammar grades, and also for any special classes, public or private, given at homes, clubs, settlements, summer schools, etc. It requires a special room equipped with suitable benches and tools. The number of children in the class should be limited to twenty.

The teacher should have training and experience, as well as a good knowledge of the correct use and care of tools and of the best methods of performing the various exercises.

The drawings, models, tools, and material are simpler than those used in the upper grades. Generally, only one view is given in the drawing, and only the necessary facts for the construction shown. The directions are brief, being intended merely as hints for methods of procedure.

While these drawings and directions are intended primarily for the use of the teacher, the children may work from them directly, after they have gained some facility in the use of tools and in the ability to read

INTRODUCTION

drawings. It should be understood, however, that no directions or drawings can take the place of the teacher.

In order to give the children a clear idea of what they are to do, the teacher should first present the model, and, by questions and explanations, lead the children to a correct understanding of both the model and its use. Enlarged blackboard drawings should be made for the children to read, and they may also be taught to make sketches and simple working drawings.

As a general rule, the method of procedure should be:

First: From the model.
Second: From model and drawing.
Third: From drawing alone.
Fourth: From the children's own suggestions guided by the teacher.

Correct working positions should be insisted upon; self-reliance and generosity should be fostered, and it must be remembered that the finished product should represent the child's own effort.

There is often a vague idea as to what is meant by the educational value of manual training. I would suggest, to make this subject clear, that, while the children are at work, the following questions should be satisfactorily answered by supervisors, teachers, or visitors:

First. Are the child's positions and movements while working such as are likely to be injurious or beneficial to his physical development?

Second. Is he doing his own thinking, unprompted and uninterrupted by the teacher?

Third. Is his work so carried on that self-respect is developed rather than vanity?

Fourth. Is he learning to recognize and to love excellence of workmanship, as shown by becoming more and more critical of himself and his own achievements?

INTRODUCTION

Fifth. Is he learning to recognize good form and to avoid unsuitable decoration?

Sixth. Is he getting some training in good citizenship by working for others?

Seventh. Does the finished product represent the child's own effort, and is the workmanship good; or was the problem too difficult?

Although the models and the directions here outlined have been planned with great care, it must be understood that they are not recommended as a fixed and unalterable plan of work. Teachers should always change the methods and models in the interest of general improvement or adapt them for special needs.

It is hoped that the suggestions here given may prove of service to teachers as well as to pupils, and meet the demand of a genuine need.

WOOD OR TIMBER

A variety of native woods suited to the character of the objects made should be selected. Wood is conceded to be superior to any other manual-training material. It has, so to speak, more life than such materials as clay, paper, or metal. The material itself excites an interest in the children. The structure or grain, as well as the great variety in coloring, gives an opportunity to study nature's way of decoration. From a physiological standpoint, also, there is no material to meet the requirements quite as adequately as wood does. It gives a measured resistance to the muscles, and can be adapted to the individual strength of the worker.

The teacher should have a good knowledge of the different kinds of wood suitable for sloyd work, especially of those kinds most easily obtained in the vicinity of the school.

The various woods are recognized by their texture, color, weight, and odor. The texture is best studied in the transverse, radial, and tangential sections. By a *transverse* or *cross* section is meant a cut across the fibres of a tree or board. A *tangential* section is cut in the direction of the fibres and at a tangent to the rings of the annual layers. A *radial* section is also made in the direction of the fibres, but forms a radius of the rings. It is this last cut which gives the beautiful figures found in oak, beech, and maple, and is commonly called quartered wood.

In studying the cross section we find in the centre a column of cellular tissue called the *pith* or *medulla*, and around this centre a number of concentric rings called the *annual layers*. By counting the number of these rings we find the age of the tree. *Heartwood* is the darker and firmer part around the pith and *sapwood* is the outer, lighter, and sappy part of the trunk. The heartwood is more fully developed, and, consequently, more durable than the sapwood. Between the bark and the last annual layer is a ring called the *Cambium*. This is in a transition state, and consists of a number of very small cells, which during spring, summer, and autumn undergo many changes in composition and form, and ultimately form a new annual ring consisting of two distinct textures known as *spring wood* and *autumn wood*. Spring wood is lighter and more porous, while autumn wood is darker and more durable. This is partly the reason for the shifting color in wood. Small lines or fibres leading from the centre to the bark are called *medullary rays* or *silver grain*. These bind together the annual layers and help in the distribution of moisture through the tree.

The best season for felling trees is during midwinter when the sap is at a standstill. By the *seasoning* of wood is meant the driving out of the sap or moisture which the wood contains. We call wood seasoned when the quantity of moisture contained coincides with that contained in the atmosphere. A fence, for example, would not need wood as well seasoned as that used for inside furniture. If too well seasoned, the wood will swell; if not sufficiently seasoned, it will shrink. We can generally tell whether wood is well seasoned by its weight. Another way of testing is by knocking on the wood, and, if it is well seasoned, it gives forth a ringing sound. Various methods of seasoning are employed. The best method is to place the wood in the open air in such a way as to permit the air to circulate freely about it. Previous to this the logs are often placed in a stream of water to draw out the sap more quickly. Another process of hastening the seasoning is by artificial means. The lumber is placed in a gradually rising temperature in a kiln, hence the name, kiln-dried wood. The rapidity with which the moisture is evaporated depends on the size and quality of the wood. Soft wood will usually dry in a kiln in four days, while hard woods take longer, some requiring years to season. The drying must always be done gradually and carefully, or the wood may split.

Lumber stored up for sloyd work should be placed in such a way that the air will circulate freely around it, that is to say, if placed on shelves, strips of wood should be placed between the boards.

Shrinking occurs whenever the wood loses moisture. The shrinkage is least with the length of the fibres, and two or three times more in a tangential than in a radial direction.

Swelling is caused by the absorption of moisture, as a drop of water placed upon a dent in a sloyd model will readily prove.

Warping is unequal shrinking or swelling.

Winding is unequal warping caused by unevenness in grain. First-class lumber is carefully selected and well seasoned, and it is this grade which is required in sloyd.

Lumber used in sloyd is generally ordered by the square foot, with a statement of kind, quality, thickness, and approximate width of boards wanted, and whether they are to be rough or planed.

The following brief description of a few kinds of common trees and woods, with the different American and Latin names, may be of interest and help to teachers and students of Elementary Sloyd and Whittling:

White Pine, Weymouth Pine, *Pinus strobus*, is one of the tallest and most stately of our evergreen trees. It sometimes reaches a height of one hundred and twenty feet, with a diameter of three to four feet. **Found** from Newfoundland to Manitoba and along the Alleghany Mountains to Georgia. **Bark** of the trunk is lighter and smoother than in the other pines. **Leaves** or needles, from three to five inches long and grow in clusters of five. **Cones,** from four to six inches long and about one inch in diameter; cylinder-shaped and slightly curved. **Wood** is valuable timber, and when freshly cut is of a creamy-white appearance, but becomes light brown on exposure. The wood is free from knots, straight-grained, and soft; not liable to warp and twist, and gives a clean, aromatic smell.

White Pine is excellent for sloyd work, but is expensive. White Wood and Bass Wood are less expensive, and may be used to some extent instead of Pine.

White Wood, Tulip Tree, *Liriodendron tulipifera*. The Tulip Tree reaches a height of one hundred and ninety feet, with a trunk ten feet in diameter. **Found** mostly as far south as Alabama and Georgia. Common in New England States, but not abundant. **Bark,** dark ash-color, furrowed. **Leaves,** alternate, simple, three to five inches long and wide. **Wood,** light, soft, straight-grained; heartwood light yellow or brown, and the thin sapwood nearly white.

Bass Wood, American Linden, Lime Tree, Bee Tree, *Tilia americana*. A straight-trunked tree, sixty to eighty feet high and two to four feet in diameter. **Found** from British America southwest to Virginia. **Bark,** very thick, dark brown. Inner bark very tough. Is used for mats and coarse rope. **Leaves,** about four to five inches long and from three to four inches wide. **Wood,** white, soft, and clear of knots, less valuable than White Wood, owing to its liability to crack in bending.

Sugar Maple, Hard Maple, Rock Maple, *Acer saccharinum*. A tree fifty to eighty feet high or more. **Found** from southern Canada through the Northern States. It grows in rich woods, often forming "groves." From its sap we get "maple sugar," about five to ten pounds from the average tree each season. **Bark,** light gray and smooth. **Leaves,** simple, opposite. **Wood** is white, uniform in texture, hard, strong, tough, and difficult to split. Accidental variations furnish the handsome Bird's-Eye Maple and Curled Maple.

Beech, *Fagus ferruginea*. A stately tree, about fifty to eighty feet high. **Found** in rich woods from Nova Scotia to Florida and westward to lower Mississippi basin. **Bark,** light gray and smooth. **Leaves,** egg-shaped, three to six inches long and about half as wide. **Fruit,** a small prickly burr, splitting half-way to the base when ripe. **Wood,** hard, close-grained, light brown, uniform in color. Medullary rays, large, glossy, and dark brown.

Sweet Gum, Bilsted, *Liquidambar styraciflua*. Sweet Gum comes from the Witch-hazel family, and is a tree sixty to one hundred feet high, with a trunk two to five feet in diameter. **Found** from Connecticut to Illinois and southward. **Bark,** light brown. In the South a spicy gum comes from the bark and is used medicinally. **Leaves,** simple, alternate, five-pointed, star-shaped, from three to five inches long and three to seven inches broad. **Wood,** bright reddish-brown, sapwood nearly white, close-grained, not strong, liable to warp in drying, easy to work, takes good polish.

Red Cedar, *Juniperus virginiana*. An evergreen tree, fifteen to thirty feet high. **Found** in southern Canada and distributed throughout the United States. **Bark,** reddish brown. **Leaves,** needle-shaped, about one-fourth of an inch long and placed in pairs, sometimes in threes. **Fruit** or berries, about the size of a small pea, bluish and covered with a white powder. **Wood,** valuable, light, durable, fragrant. Heartwood dull red, sapwood white. Used almost exclusively in the making of lead pencils.

Butternut, White Walnut, *Juglans cinerea*. Common. Usually fifty to seventy feet high. **Bark,** light grayish-brown. **Leaves,** alternate, compound, fifteen to thirty inches long, with eleven to seventeen leaflets. **Fruit,** nut, rough, nearly cylindrical; one-half to two and a half inches long. Kernel sweet, but oily. **Wood,** light brown, light, soft. Coarse-grained and not strong. Takes good polish.

Black Walnut, *Juglans nigra*. This is one of the grandest and most massive trees. It reaches a height of sixty to seventy feet. Generally distributed, abundant in the middle of the Mississippi Valley. **Bark,** dark brown. **Leaves,** alternate, compound, from one to two feet long. Fifteen to twenty-three leaflets. **Fruit,** nut, oval. About one and one-half inches in length. Kernel sweet and edible. **Wood,** dark purplish-brown, heavy, hard, close-grained, and strong. Takes a beautiful polish.

The Redwood, *Sequoia sempervirens.* The Redwood of California is a coniferous tree and belongs to a genus of which the Big Tree is the only other species now alive. Redwood forms dense forests on the west slopes of the Coast Range. It grows to a greater height than any other American tree. It reaches a height of from two hundred and twenty-five to three hundred and fifty feet, with a diameter of from ten to twenty feet. Most of the Redwood cut are from four hundred to eight hundred years old. The oldest Redwood found began life one thousand three hundred and seventy-three years ago. **Bark** is of a reddish-gray color. **Wood** is of color that shades from light cherry to dark mahogany. It is used for all kinds of finishing and construction lumber. Usually straight-grained, light, firm, yet soft. The wood is durable, easy to work, and takes a good polish. This wood is not much used in the Eastern market, owing largely to the high freight-rates in shipping.

SUPPLEMENTARY READING ON TREES FOR THE TEACHER.

"Our Native Trees," by Harriet L. Keeler, Charles Scribner's Sons, New York.
"American Woods," by Romeyn Hough, Lowville, N. Y.
"The Trees of North-Eastern America," by Charles S. Newhall.
"Timber," Bulletin No. 10, United States Department of Agriculture, Division of Forestry.
"The Redwood," Bulletin No. 38, U. S. Department of Agriculture, Bureau of Forestry.
"With the Trees," by Maud Going, comments on the trees from the standpoints of the naturalist and nature-lover, and contains legends and stories.
"A Year with Trees," by Wilson Flagg; gives brief essays on trees and their habits, and considers the tree in its relation to climate, soil, birds, insects, ornament, poetry, and fable.
"A Guide to the Trees," by Alice Lounsberry; brief descriptions of trees from the standpoint of the naturalist, with some notes of legend and history. Especially fine illustrations in color by Mrs. Ellis Rowan.
"Familiar Trees," by F. Schuyler Matthews; a naturalist's description of trees.

"Among Flowers and Trees with the Poets," compiled by Minnie Curtis Wait and Merton Channing Leonard. Parts III and IV of this volume are devoted to trees and shrubs—in general; trees and shrubs—specified. This book contains a rare collection of flower and tree poetry.

"In the Child's World," by Emilie Poulsson; list of tree selections for teachers is given on page 256.

SUPPLEMENTARY READING ON TREES FOR CHILDREN

The following list of books for children contains facts about trees, descriptions of trees and their habits, as well as stories, myths, and legends in prose and poetry. Most of the volumes are illustrated.

"Trees in Prose and Poetry," by Gertrude L. Stone and Grace Frichett. This book presents the tree in descriptive narrative and in legend, myth, and story.

"Book of Nature Myths," by Florence Holbrook, contains two legends: "Why the Evergreen Trees Never Lose Their Leaves" and "Why the Aspen Leaves Tremble."

"Nature Myths," by Flora J. Cooke, contains the following tree stories: "Daphne," "Fairy Story," "Philemon and Baucis," "Poplar Tree," "The Secret of Fire."

"In Mythland," by M. Helen Beckwith, contains two tree stories: "How Daphne Became a Tree"; "Philemon and Baucis."

"The Stories Mother Nature Told her Children," by Jane Andrews, contains two tree stories: "The Talk of the Trees in the Village Street," "How Quercus Alba went to Explore the Under World and What Came of It."

"The Stories of the Trees," by Mrs. Dyson, presents, in a series of talks, the natural features and habits of trees, as well as various historical facts relating to them.

"A Japanese Garland," by Florence Peltier, gives the Japanese symbolism of tree and flower.

"The Story Hour," by K. D. Wiggin and Nora A. Smith, contains "A Story of the Forest," a charming Xmas story.

"Stories," by Hans C. Andersen, contains "The Last Dream of the Old Oak," a symbolic tree story in Andersen's best vein.

"In the Child's World," by Emilie Poulsson, gives talks and poems on trees, pages 253–262. In this volume a list of tree selections is given for teacher and children. Page 30 contains a charming story, "An Old-Fashioned Rhyme, 'This Is the Tree of the Forest.'"

"Nature in Verse," compiled by Mary I. Lovejoy. "Three Trees," page 288; "The Little Pine Tree," page 285; "The Tree," by Björnson, page 26; "The Tree," by Jones Very, page 27.

"Open Sesame," vol. 1. Edited by B. W. Bellamy and M. D. Goodwin. "To the Fir Tree," from the German, page 121.

"All the Year Round." Part II. "Winter," compiled by Frances L. Strong; "The Little Fir Trees," page 56; by Evaleen Stein; "The Fir Tree," adapted from Andersen, page 50; "The Discontented Pine," by C. S. Bumstead, page 46; "The Evergreen," page 42; "The Pine," page 44.

"Golden Numbers," compiled by Kate D. Wiggin and Nora A. Smith; "The Planting of the Apple Tree," page 59, Bryant; "Mine Host of the Golden Apple," page 64, Thomas Westwood; "A Young Fir Tree," D. G. Rossetti, page 65; "The Showing of the Pines," page 66, by T. W Higginson.

TOOLS AND IMPLEMENTS FOR ELEMENTARY SLOYD

TOOLS are instruments by which the hands give material expression to thought. Consequently, such tools should be selected as will best promote physical and mental growth.

The tools should be of the best quality; although the first cost may seem large it is cheaper in the long run. While tools of regular size are best in ordinary sloyd, smaller ones should be selected for young children. Toy tools, or those found in children's tool-boxes, are generally of poor quality and not to be recommended. To avoid many failures, the tools should not only be of the right kind, but properly sharpened and adjusted. It must be remembered that good tools must be kept in good condition.

To teach habits of order and neatness, Benches and Tools must be kept in perfect order. The rule should be: "A place for everything and everything in its place."

In order to simplify and economize the outfit for Elementary Sloyd, it is thought best that only one kind of Plane be used, and that such tools as Marking Gauges, Auger Bits, Chisels, and Carving Tools be excluded.

The following illustrations, with explanations of Benches and Tools used in Elementary Sloyd, may be of service:

Fig. 1.

SINGLE ADJUSTABLE SLOYD BENCH

The Bench here illustrated was designed by the author in 1889. It differs from the ordinary carpenter's bench in that it is adjustable to suit the height of the worker. Instead of the common iron bench-stop for planing, it has an end vise and holes for wooden stops or pins along the bench-top. These hold the wood securely at both ends while planing bevels, cylinders, etc., and in modelling different forms. A single stop may be used for straight-surface planing. As a general rule, such work as requires strong muscular effort should be done in the direction of the length of the bench, and any hammering or pounding should be done over the upright supports. The top is glued up from four or more strips of maple to prevent warping, and the lower part is fastened together by keyed joints. Vises and screws are made of maple. Wood screws are considered better, although iron screws will be furnished if desired.

Two sizes of this Bench are made. The smaller size is designated by the manufacturers as No. 6, and is large enough for any work which may be done by children in grammar grades.

The extreme length and width of Bench No. 6 is forty-two by twenty-eight inches, and Bench No. 5 is one foot longer. The height may be adjusted from thirty to thirty-three inches, which is suitable for pupils from eight to twelve years.

The Benches should be placed in such a way as to have the light come from the left and back as the worker faces the Bench.

The distance between Benches should not be less than two feet. Benches should be securely fastened to the floor by means of a leg screw at each end.

Tools most frequently used are kept on the bench, in racks, and on hooks, all within sight. This arrangement allows the teacher to observe readily the order in which the tools are kept, and in this respect it is superior to the use of drawers and lockers. The back-board with the tool-rack may be lowered, if desired, so as to make it level with the bench-top. Great care should be taken not to injure the bench-top. To keep it in good condition it should be rubbed down occasionally with raw linseed oil.

ELEMENTARY SLOYD AND WHITTLING

Fig. 2.

WORK TABLE FOR FOUR PUPILS

This Table is designed for use in places where the regular single sloyd bench is thought too expensive. It is a strong Table. Size of top, thirty-six by thirty-six inches; height, thirty inches; four vises attached. This accommodates four pupils.

ELEMENTARY SLOYD AND WHITTLING

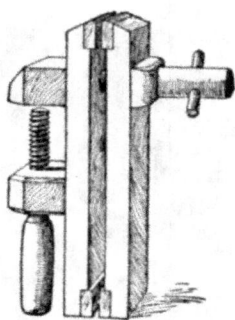

Fig. 3.

CLAMP VISE

In order further to lessen the expense of an outfit, Clamp Vises may be obtained and fastened to a horizontal board or strong table. This clamp can be used only while doing light work.

Tools illustrated in the order in which they are used:

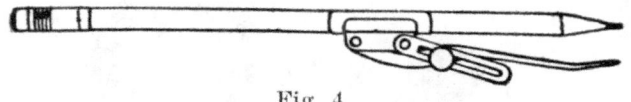

Fig. 4.

NEW PENCIL COMPASSES

Lead pencil No. 3 is recommended for wood-work. Keep point of pencil about one inch long. In sharpening, remove wood with knife and point the lead on No. 1 sandpaper.

In using Compasses adjust point to equal length with pencil point and hold at top between thumb and forefinger.

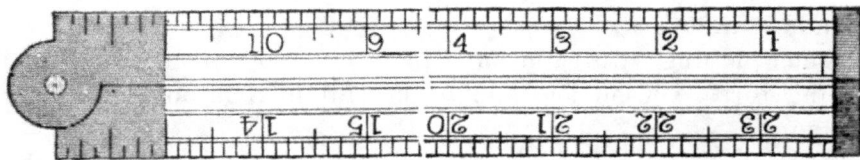

Fig. 5.

RULE (BOXWOOD, 2 FT. 2 FOLD)

Hold Rule on edge in measuring and marking distances, but lay it flat on material in drawing lines.

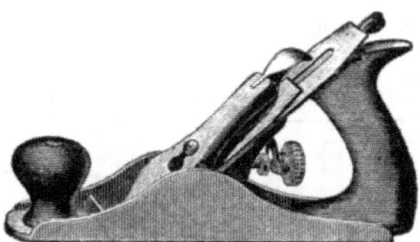

Fig. 6.

IRON SMOOTHING-PLANE, 8 IN. X 1 3-4 IN. CUTTER (BAILEY)

Set Cap-iron about one-sixteenth of an inch from edge of Plane-iron. Adjust plane iron for coarse or fine shavings by using the thumb on the brass adjusting-nut (thumb-screw) while resting the "heel" on the bench. Move lateral adjustment so as to make edge of Plane-iron appear even.

Grasp the plane by the handle and press and guide firmly with the other hand on the "knob," taking special care not to tip the plane at the ends of the wood.

When planing with right hand place left foot forward in direction of working force. Keep legs and back straight, but not in a constrained position.

When end planing on bench hook is to be done, set cap back about one-eighth of an inch, and hold side of plane firmly on the bench close to bench hook.

If plane clogs with shavings remove iron to clean it. Never take out shavings with knife or any other tool. In grinding or whetting plane-iron keep cutting-edge and bevel straight, rounding the corners a little.

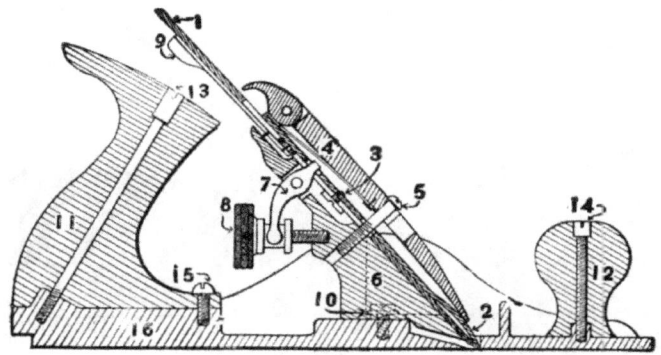

Fig. 7.

LIST OF PARTS OF BAILEY PLANE

1. Plane-Iron.
2. Plane-Iron Cap.
3. Plane-Iron Screw.
4. Cap.
5. Cap Screw.
6. Frog.
7. "Y" Adjustment.
8. Brass Adjusting-Nut or Thumb-screw.
9. Lateral Adjustment.
10. Frog Screw.
11. Handle.
12. Knob.
13. Handle "Bolt and Nut."
14. Knob "Bolt and Nut."
15. Handle Screw.
16. Bottom.

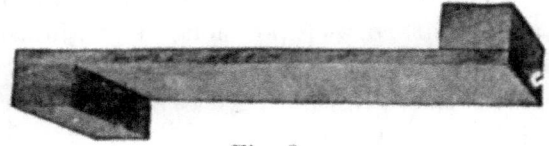

Fig. 8.

BENCH-HOOK, OAK

Examine Bench-hook with try square to see if it is true. If not, correct it before using. Hook it over edge of bench or fasten in vise flat and firmly.

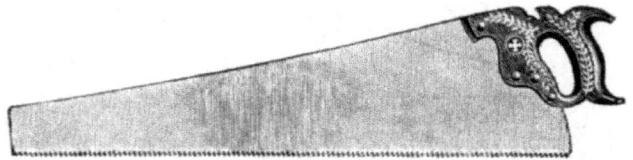

Fig. 9.

SPLITTING SAW (SPECIAL, 14 IN. 10 PTS.)

This Saw is used for sawing with the grain of the wood, or in the direction in which the wood splits. The cutting-off or cross-cut Saw is used for cutting across the fibres of the wood. For shape of different teeth see Fig. 10.

The Saw should be grasped firmly with one hand on handle and the other resting on the wood. Place the feet in proper position, with the advance foot in the direction of the working force, as in planing. The saw must not be pressed down upon the wood, but moved horizontally with long, light, and even strokes.

NOTE: In the vigorous exercises of planing and sawing, it is of the utmost importance that correct positions be maintained, in order to avoid fatigue and possible deformity, and to insure better work. For the same reasons exercises in planing, sawing, and boring may be done alternately by right and left hand.

Splitting 10 pts. to inch.

Cutting off 12 pts. to inch.

Fig. 10.

SAW TEETH

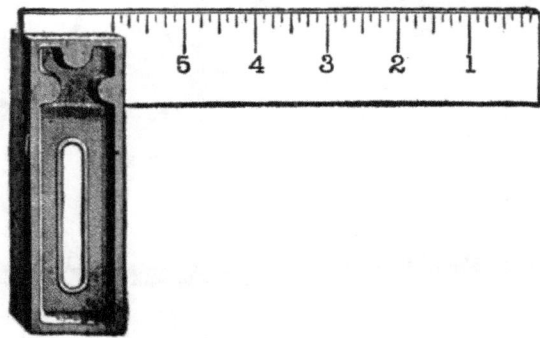

Fig. 11.

IRON HANDLE TRY SQUARE

This tool consists of blade and beam or handle, and is used for testing surfaces which should be at right angles to each other, and for spuaring lines across the wood. In using hold the handle firmly up to the planed face (working face) of the wood. Do not hammer or pry with this tool, as it makes it inaccurate for use.

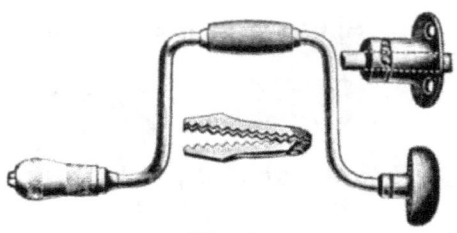

Fig. 12.

BIT BRACE (BARBER, 4 IN.)

Fasten the bit securely in the jaws. When using hold the head of the brace in the left hand and turn crank to right.

Fig. 13.

DRILL BIT, WITH BIT POINT

This bit is used for boring holes for nails, screws, etc. This tool has a triangular point to insure its boring in the right place. Be careful to hold bit at right angles to wood and use light, even pressure. Boring in a horizontal direction is preferable in Elementary Sloyd.

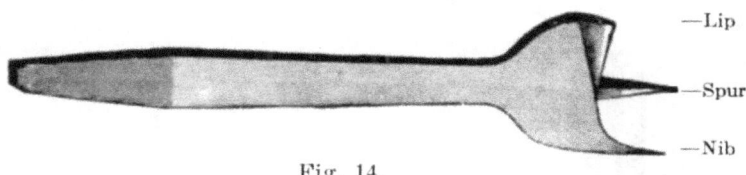

Fig. 14.

CENTRE BIT

This tool is useful for boring in thin wood, as it does not split it. Bore only until the centre or spur comes through, then turn wood and finish.

The bit should be sharpened with a fine file and slip stone and tried on waste piece of wood before using.

Fig. 15.

COUNTERSINK (ROSE)

This tool is used with brace to sink holes for screw heads.

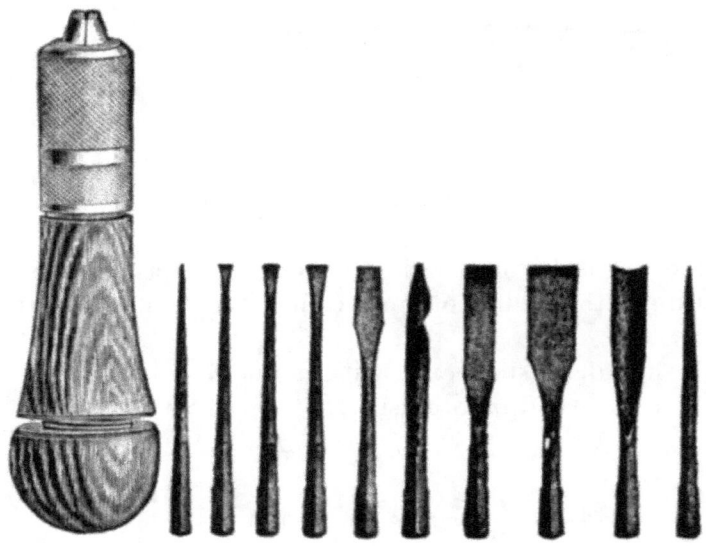

Fig. 16.

TOOL HANDLE WITH 20 AWLS AND TOOLS

The cuts of this tool illustrate the various uses for which it is adapted.

In using the brad-awl place the edge across the grain of the wood and repeatedly turn the hand half-way around and back with slight pressure.

Fig. 17.

BACK SAW, 10 INCH

This is a saw with very fine teeth and makes a smooth cut. In Elementary Sloyd it may be used in place of the cross-cut saw.

The thin blade is strengthened by an iron "back," from which the saw derives its name.

Fig. 18.

HAMMER, A. E. B. F. (7 OZ.)

Hold the hammer near the end of handle and strike squarely on the nail head. When withdrawing nails with the claw of the hammer place a block of wood under the head so as not to injure the planed surface.

Fig. 19.

NAIL SET (HOLLOW POINT)

The nail set is used for driving nails below the surface of the wood. The hole left in the wood after setting the nail may be partly closed by applying a drop of water, but no putty or plug should be used. The nail set with the hollow point is preferable to the one with a flat point, as it does not slip.

Fig. 20.

HALF ROUND FILE, 8 IN.

A file should never be used when an edge tool can accomplish the work.

In smoothing a surface to a line hold the handle of the file with the right hand and place the left hand at the end of the file, with the thumb on the top. If the file becomes clogged, use a file card or place in lukewarm water. After drying clean with a brush.

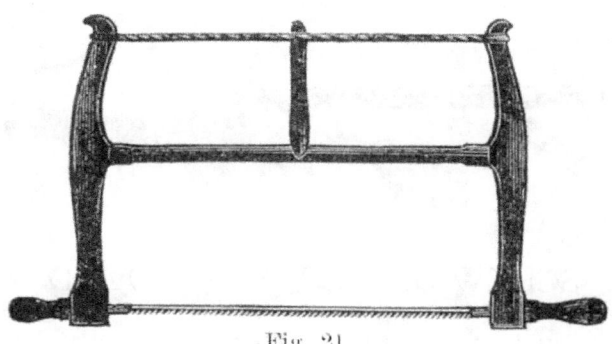

Fig. 21.

TURNING SAW (8 IN., 1-8 IN. BLADE, 12 PTS.)

Before using the turning saw, see that the blade is perfectly straight and tight. Grasp the saw with both hands at the handle where the teeth of the saw point away from you and move it squarely through the wood with long, light, steady strokes. By loosening the cord and taking out one end of the blade it may be used for interior cutting, such as picture-frames, etc.

Fig. 22.

IRON SPOKE-SHAVE

The spoke-shave is a most valuable tool because both hands are equally used. Originally it was used in making spokes, hence its name. It can be used either from you or towards you, but always on curved surfaces and should not be used where the plane can be used equally well. Care must be taken to cut always with the grain of the wood.

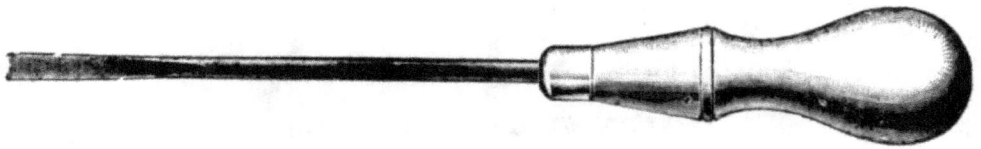

Fig. 23.

SCREW-DRIVER, 3-IN. ROUND

See that the end of the screw-driver is perfectly flat and that the narrow sides are as nearly parallel as possible. In using hold it firmly and straight in the groove of the screw head, so as not to mar the screw head.

Fig. 24.

SLOYD KNIFE, 3-IN. BLADE

The knife is not recommended for Elementary Sloyd, as children may not have sufficient strength for its use. It is a useful tool, however, in places where no other can be used conveniently. The knife recommended has a blade three inches long, with a straight bevel on both sides and a four-inch handle. The tang of the blade is riveted through the handle so as to make it more secure.

Fig. 25.

COMPASS SAW (IRON HANDLE)

The compass or keyhole saw is used to saw interior parts, such as keyholes, picture-frames, etc.

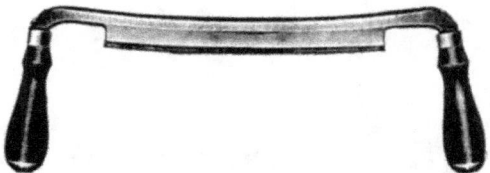

Fig. 26.

DRAWING KNIFE

This tool, like the spoke-shave, can be used with both hands. It is used for heavy work in cutting off rough edges, branches and bark, rounding poles, handles, etc. In using the drawing knife the wood should be fastened in the vise.

Fig. 27

FLAT FILE, SMOOTH, 5 IN.

This file is used for sharpening bits, cap irons, etc., previous to the use of the slip stone.

Fig. 28.

SLIP STONE

The slip stone is used for whetting the inside of gouges, bits, etc.

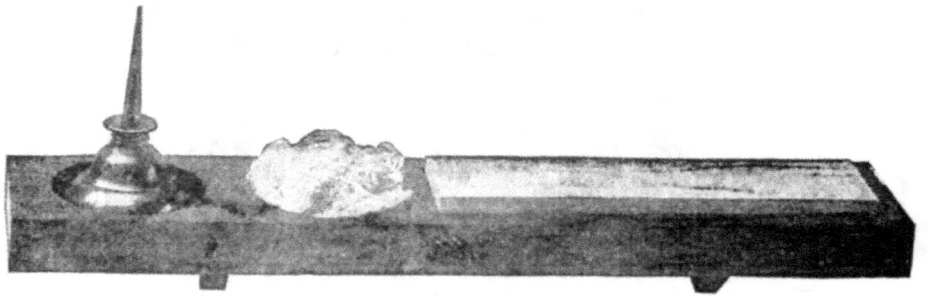

Fig. 29.

SHARPENING OUTFIT

The oil stone should be kept clean and straight. If uneven it is difficult to sharpen the tools properly.

To make the oil stone level fasten a half sheet of No. 1 sandpaper on a board, apply a little water, and rub until true.

Fig. 30.

GRINDSTONE, 18-IN. DIAMETER

Keep water in the trough only when grinding. In sharpening edge tools turn the stone toward the edge of the tool. Hold the tool steadily and firmly and give a lateral motion across the stone to prevent irregular wearing.

Aim to make a flat bevel.

For the illustration of tools, the author is indebted to Messrs. Chandler & Barber, Boston, Mass.

ELEMENTARY SLOYD AND WHITTLING

LIST OF TOOLS AND MATERIAL FOR FOUR PUPILS

1 Work Table for four pupils, $10.
  Single Adjustable Sloyd Bench, $9.
4 New Pencil Compasses, with Lead Pencil No. 3.
4 Rules (boxwood, 2 foot, 2 fold).
4 Iron Smoothing Planes, 8 x $1\frac{3}{4}$ inch cutter (Bailey).
4 Bench Hooks.
2 Splitting Saws (special 14 inches, 10 points).
4 Try Squares, (6 inches).
2 Bit Braces (Barber, 4 inches).
2 Drill Bits, with bit points each 3-16 and $\frac{1}{4}$ inch.
2 Centre Bits, each, $\frac{3}{4}$, $\frac{5}{8}$, $\frac{1}{2}$, $\frac{3}{8}$, and $\frac{1}{4}$ inch.
1 Countersink (Rose).
1 Tool Handle (20 awls and tools).
2 Back Saws, (10 inches).
1 Hammer, A. E. B. F. (7 ounces).
1 Nail Set (hollow point).
2 Half Round Files (8 inches).
2 Turning Saws (8 inches, $\frac{1}{8}$-inch blade, 12 points).
2 Iron Spoke-shaves.
1 Screw-driver (3 inches round).
2 Sloyd Knives (3-inch blade).
1 Cross-cut Saw (special, 14 inches).
1 Compass Saw (iron handle).
Total cost for one pupil with single Adjustable Bench, $20.
Total cost for four pupils with table for four, $33.19.

AMOUNT OF WOOD FOR THE FIRST TWELVE MODELS FOR FOUR PUPILS

The wood should be of the best quality, kiln-dried and planed.

4 square feet $\frac{1}{4}$- inch Whitewood.
7 " " $\frac{3}{8}$- " "
3 " " $\frac{1}{2}$- " "
10 " " $\frac{5}{8}$- " "
$\frac{1}{4}$ " foot $\frac{7}{8}$- " "
1 " " $\frac{5}{8}$- " White Pine.
6 " feet $\frac{1}{4}$- " Sweet Gum or Black Walnut.
$1\frac{1}{2}$ " " $\frac{3}{8}$- " " " " " "
4 Maple Dowels $\frac{5}{8}$ inch.

MISCELLANEOUS

Wire Brads $\frac{1}{2}$ inch, No 19.
" " 1 " No 17.
" " $1\frac{1}{2}$ inches, No. 15.
Screws $\frac{3}{8}$ inch, No. 1.
" 1 " No. 8.
" $1\frac{1}{4}$ inches, No. 10 (Round Head).
" 2 " No. 14 (Round Head, Blue).
$\frac{1}{2}$ Pint Le Page's Liquid Glue.
Sandpaper Nos. 1 and 0.
Flat File. (Smooth, 5 inch.)
Slip Stone.
Sharpening Outfit (India Oil Stone, Oil Can, and Cotton Waste, mounted on wood).
Grindstone 18 inches diameter.

ELEMENTARY SLOYD

DIRECTIONS FOR ELEMENTARY SLOYD

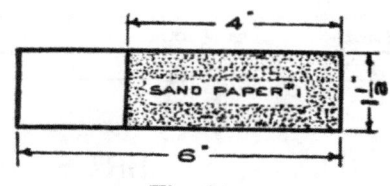

Fig. 31.

1.—PENCIL SHARPENER
Whitewood. ¼ inch.

TOOLS
Pencil, Rule, Plane, Bench Hook.

DIRECTIONS
Wood prepared $6\frac{1}{8}$ x $1\frac{3}{4}$ inches.

1. Plane one side straight.
2. Measure width, draw line, and plane.
3. Plane one end in bench hook.
4. Measure length and plane.
5. Sandpaper with block, rounding corners.
6. Cut sandpaper, No. 1, and glue to wood.

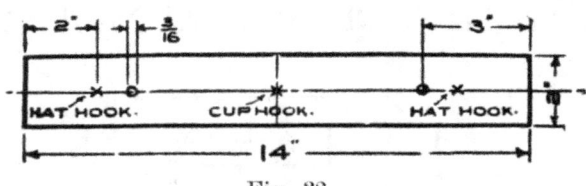

Fig. 32.

2.—HAT AND BRUSH RACK
White Pine. ⅜ inch.

NEW TOOLS
Splitting Saw, Try Square, Bit Brace, and Drill Bit.

DIRECTIONS
Wood prepared in length 14¼ inches.

1. Plane one side straight and square.
2. Measure width, draw line, saw ⅛ inch from it, and plane to line.
3. See 3 and 4 in Model No. 1.
4. Draw centre line, measure for hooks and holes, and bore holes.
5. See 5 in Model No. 1.
6. Put in hooks, two wire hooks for ends and one cup hook for centre.

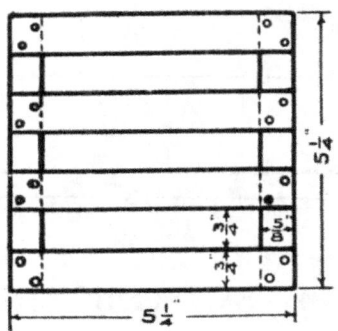

Fig. 33.

3.—STAND

Whitewood. ¼ and ⅜ inch.

NEW TOOLS
Back Saw, Hammer, and Nail Set.

DIRECTIONS
Wood for supports 11 x ⅜ inch, for slats 11 x ¼ inch.

1. Saw for supports 1 inch wide and plane square to required dimensions.
2. Find centre, saw with back saw.
3. See 3 and 4, Model No. 1.
4. Saw pieces for slats 1 inch wide, and plane and saw as for supports.
5. Sandpaper, find points for nails, drive and set nails.

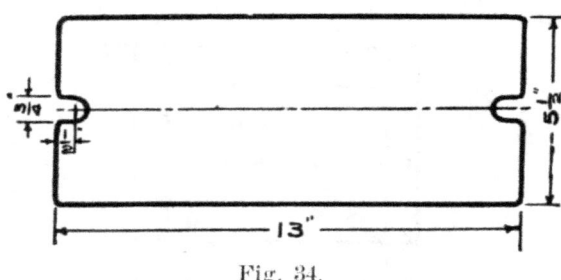

Fig. 34.

4.—SWING BOARD

Whitewood.   ⅝ inch.

NEW TOOLS

Centre Bit ¾ inch, half-round File 8 inches.

DIRECTIONS

Wood prepared in length 13¼ inches.

1. See 1 and 2 in Model No. 2.
2. Fasten wood firmly in the vise and plane one end square. (In order not to split corners, always plane from corners toward centre.)
3. Measure length, draw line, and plane to it.
4. Find points for centres of holes, and bore (horizontally) from both sides.
5. Draw lines with try square, finish with back saw, file, and sandpaper.

NOTE: See that centre bit is well sharpened with file and slip stone and tried before using.

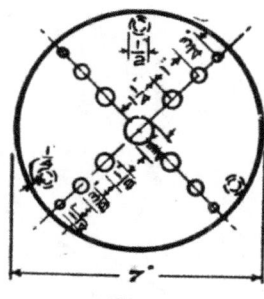

Fig. 35.

5.—TEAPOT STAND

Whitewood. ⅜ inch.

NEW TOOLS

Pencil Compasses, Turning Saw, Spoke-shave, Screw-driver, ½-inch. Centre Bit with lip filed away is used in making the feet.

DIRECTIONS

Wood prepared $7\frac{1}{2}$ x $7\frac{1}{2}$ inches.

1. Draw one diagonal. Erect perpendicular at centre and draw circle.
2. Fasten wood firmly in vise, keeping grain of wood nearly in a vertical position to avoid splitting.
3. Saw $\frac{1}{8}$ inch outside of circle, holding saw firmly with both hands at handle end of blade. Care should be taken to keep blade at right angles to surface of wood.
4. Spoke-shave to line, always using the tool with the grain of the wood.
5. Locate centres for holes and bore.
6. Sandpaper, make feet of ¼-inch wood, and fasten with ½-inch screws.

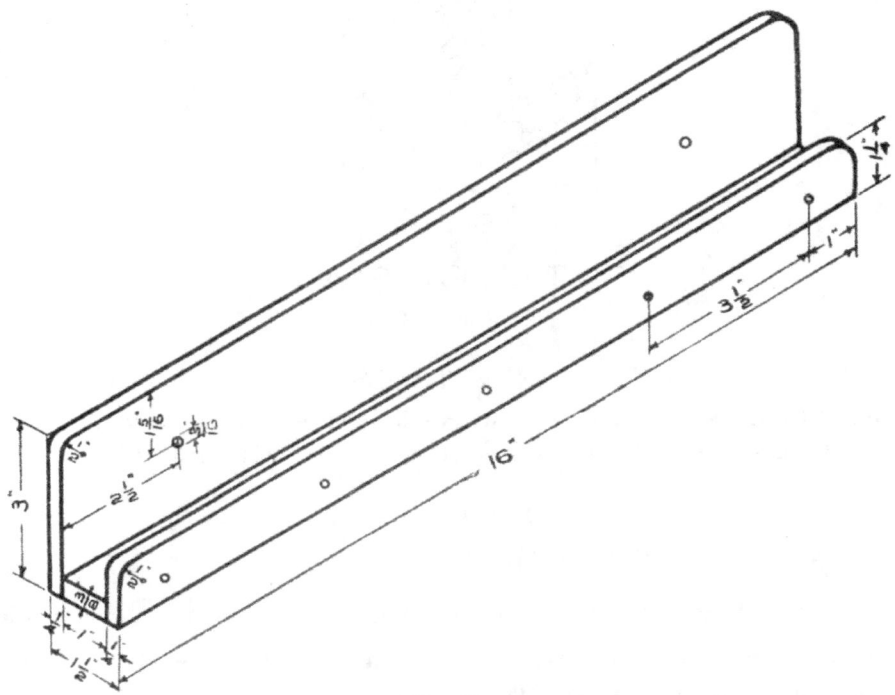

Fig. 36.

6.—SHELF FOR PHOTOGRAPHS
Whitewood. ¼ and ½ inch.

NEW TOOLS
Cross-cut Saw and Knife.

ELEMENTARY SLOYD AND WHITTLING

DIRECTIONS

1. Let pupil estimate the proper amount of wood.
2. Explain and illustrate to children the difference between cross-cut and splitting saws.
3. Saw with cross-cut and splitting saws.
4. Plane pieces to required dimensions.
5. Draw arcs with compasses, cut to line with knife, and finish with file.
6. Locate points for holes and nails.
7. Bore-holes, sandpaper, nail, and set nails.

NOTE: Simple decoration, such as punching, veining, or coloring, may be used on front of shelf at the discretion of the teacher.

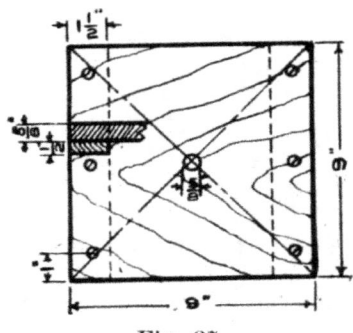

Fig. 37.

7.—RING TOSS

Whitewood. ⅝ and ⅞ inch, ⅝-inch dowel.

NEW TOOL
Countersink.

DIRECTIONS
See 1, 3, and 4 in Model No. 6.

1. If a bevel is desired, draw lines and plane.
2. Locate holes for screws and for dowel.
3. Bore with centre bit and drill bit.
4. Countersink holes for screws, sandpaper, and fasten cleats to board across the grain of the wood.
5. Fit and glue dowel.

NOTE: The rings may be made of rope, rattan, or wire wound with raffia, or bought ready for use.

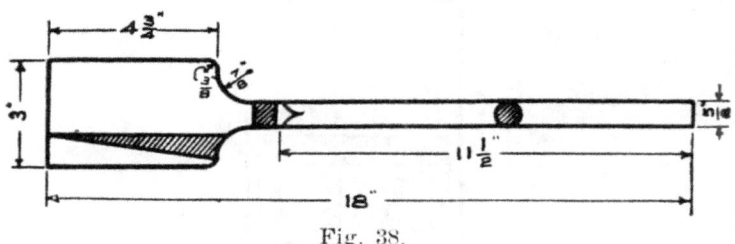

Fig. 38.

8.—SPADE

Whitewood. Thickness, ⅜ inch.

DIRECTIONS

1. See 1, 3, and 4 in Model No. 6.
2. Measure and draw on wood straight lines and arcs for handle and blade.
3. Bore holes and saw with splitting saw and back saw.
4. Finish to lines with knife and spoke-shave.
5. Draw oblique lines on sides of blade, and plane.
6. Round handle (making it first octagonal) with spoke-shave, finish with file, and sandpaper.

ELEMENTARY SLOYD AND WHITTLING

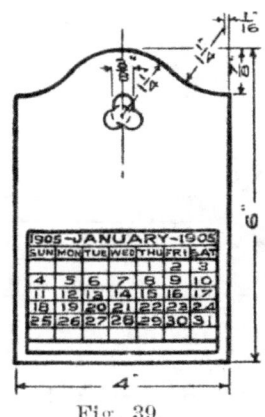

Fig. 39.

9.—CALENDAR BACK

Sweet Gum or Black Walnut. ¼ inch.

DIRECTIONS

1. Prepare wood 7 inches long, and plane to correct width.
2. Draw centre line and construction for top.
3. Finish with turning saw, knife, and file.
4. Bore holes with ⅜-inch centre bit, beginning with lower **left-hand** hole.
5. Mark length, saw, and plane.
6. Finish with sandpaper and mount calendar.

NOTE: This back may also be used in constructing a match-safe.

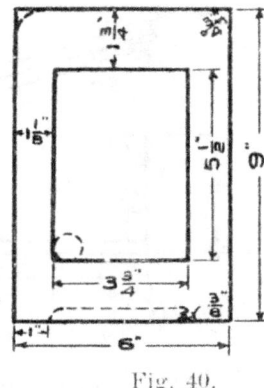

Fig. 40.

10.—FRAME

Sweet Gum or Black Walnut.   ¼ inch.

NEW TOOL
Compass Saw.

DIRECTIONS

1. Prepare oblong.
2. Draw lines for opening.
3. Place centres for ¾-inch holes at corners and bore.
4. Use compass saw, and saw close to line.
5. Finish with knife, file, and sandpaper.

NOTE: Size of frame according to the picture suggested by the children. Cardboard may be used for the back. The frame may be finished to dotted lines if desired.

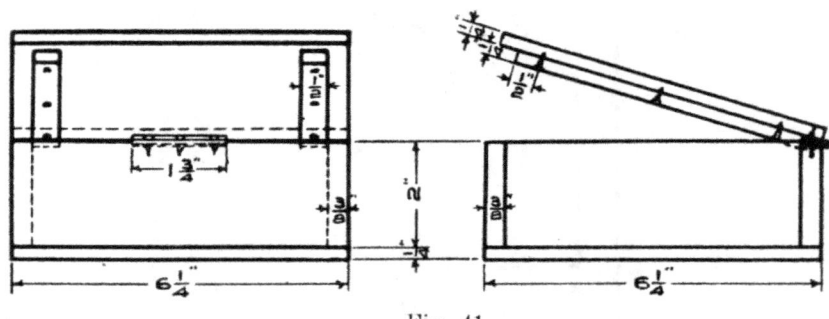

Fig. 41.

11.—HANDKERCHIEF BOX

Sweet Gum or Black Walnut.   ⅜ and ¼ inch.

DIRECTIONS

1. Prepare sides in one piece and finish to required dimensions.
2. Sandpaper inside and nail, using 1-inch brads.
3. Prepare cover and bottom in one piece and finish to required dimensions.
4. Sandpaper bottom and nail.
5. Prepare cleats and screw to cover.
6. Fit hinges (1½ inch narrow) and sink to proper depth on box only, screw hinge to box, and then to cover. A simple fastener may be attached.

NOTE: Appropriate decorations, such as simple carving, burning, or coloring, may be applied on Models 9, 10, and 11.

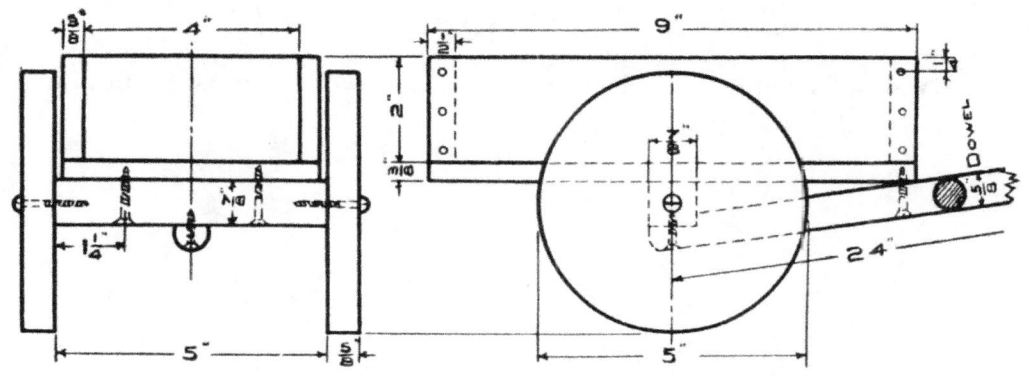

Fig. 42.

12.—CART

Whitewood. ¼, ⅜, and ⅞ inch. Maple Dowel ⅝ x 24 inches.

DIRECTIONS

1. Prepare sides and bottom in one piece, and the ends in similar manner.
2. Finish separate parts and nail box together, using 1¼-inch brads for sides and 1-inch brads for bottom.
3. Prepare pieces for wheels and finish with turning saw, spoke-shave, and file.
4. Prepare axle and use ⅝-inch dowel for handle.
5. Bore holes in sides of axle, in handle, and wheels, and fasten screws in same order. Use round-head blue screws (2 inch No. 14) for wheels, and flat-head screws (1⅛ inch No. 10) for axle and handle.

SUPPLEMENTARY MODELS

By supplementary models is meant a variety of objects containing given exercises to suit individual needs.

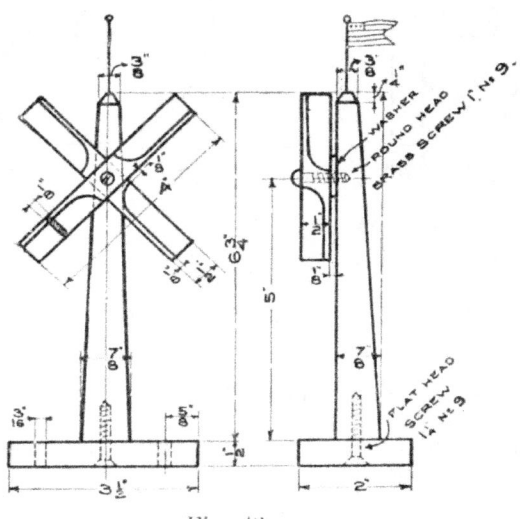

Fig. 43.

TOY WINDMILL
White Pine. ⅞ and ½ inch.

DIRECTIONS

1. Make base according to drawing.
2. Make upright support 6¾ x ⅞ inches square.
3. Plane one end square in bench hook.

ELEMENTARY SLOYD AND WHITTLING

4. Taper with plane on three sides to $\frac{3}{8}$-inch square at top.
5. Make "wings" in one length $8\frac{1}{4} \times \frac{1}{2}$ inch square.
6. Measure, square lines, cut in halves, and plane ends in bench hook to required length.
7. Measure, square lines on three sides of each piece, for halved together joint.
8. Make joint with back saw and knife, taking care to fit it tight and put together.
9. Draw one diagonal at each end in opposite directions.
10. Measure and draw curved and straight lines on both sides of each "wing" according to drawing.
11. Take joint apart and finish "wings" with knife and sandpaper.
12. Press joint together and bore holes through it and the base with $\frac{3}{16}$-inch drill bit.
13. Make a round washer of wood $\frac{1}{2} \times \frac{1}{8}$ inch.
14. Sandpaper, insert washer, and screw parts together.
15. Insert a wire at top with a light flag which will indicate direction of the wind. Fasten base in a windy place with two screws and turn upright support according to the direction of the wind.

NOTE: A more complicated windmill which would set in motion some mechanical apparatus may be constructed.

ELEMENTARY SLOYD AND WHITTLING

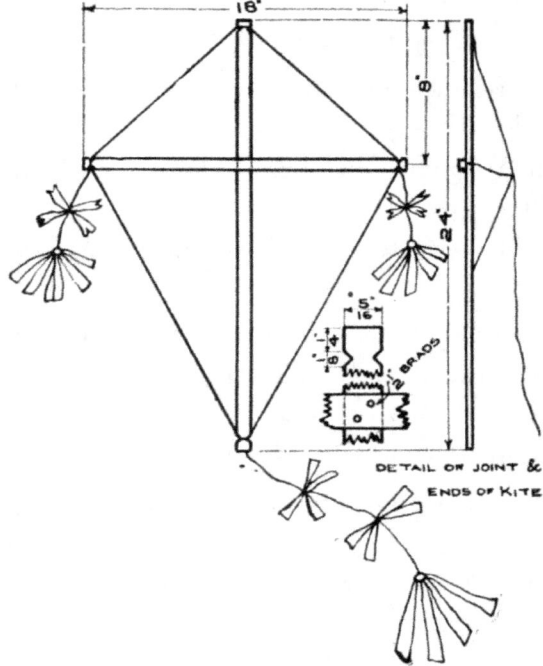

Fig. 44.

KITE

Whitewood. ¼ inch.

DIRECTIONS

1. Prepare with saw and plane two strips of wood, one $24 \times \frac{5}{16}$ inches and the other $18 \times \frac{5}{16}$ inches.
2. Cut notches at ends with knife according to drawing.
3. Measure and join pieces together by means of two $\frac{1}{2}$-inch brads.

4. Sink brads with nail-set, holding the wood on a piece of metal, and strengthen joint by winding and tying a string crosswise around.
5. Use light but strong twine around the kite, tying it securely at each end.
6. Cover with light paper or cambric by folding and pasting or gluing it around the string.
7. Fasten a piece of twine about a foot long at each side, and cut and tie paper wings to it.
8. Make tail about three times as long as length of kite and fasten light paper wings on it about 8 inches apart.
9. Fasten the end of a ball or spool of strong twine to kite, according to drawing, and in flying use a reel to wind it on.

NOTE: Different sizes and shapes of kites may be made, but the one described above will prove to be simple and to fly well.

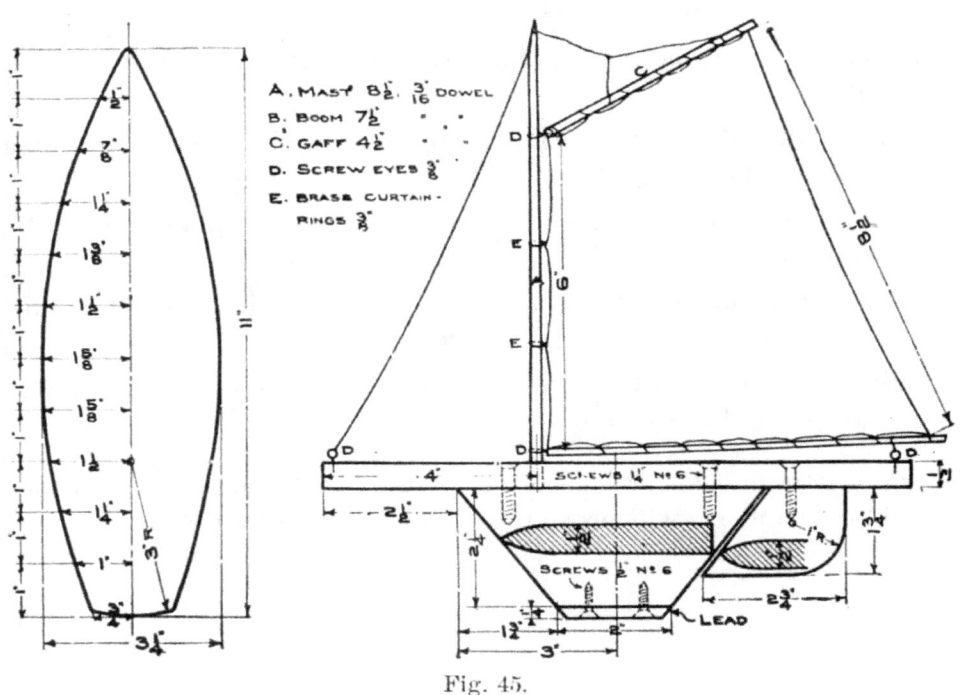

Fig. 45.

TOY BOAT

White Pine. ½ inch.

DIRECTIONS

1. Prepare wood 11½ x 3½ inches.
2. Plane one side straight.
3. Draw centre line parallel to planed side.
4. Divide distances of length and square lines across.

ELEMENTARY SLOYD AND WHITTLING

5. Measure and mark distances of width and connect points with a free-hand curve.
6. Draw arc at end with compass.
7. Cut to lines with turning saw and finish with spoke-shave and knife.
8. Make keel and rudder according to drawing.
9. Fasten keel and rudder with screws.
10. Prepare lead for keel and fasten with screws.
11. Use $\frac{3}{16}$-inch maple dowel for mast, boom, and gaff.
12. Make sail and rig according to drawing.
13. Try boat in bath-tub to see if it balances.

NOTE: If children have the requisite skill, use thicker wood for hull and hollow it out with gouge and shape it outside with spoke-shave. Various sizes may be made.

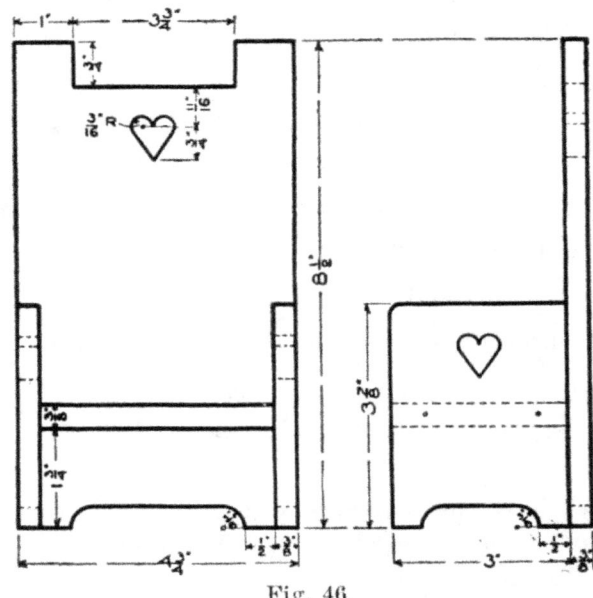

Fig. 46.

DOLL'S CHAIR

Whitewood. ⅜ inch.

DIRECTIONS

1. Prepare an oblong for back according to the drawing.
2. Saw out side pieces and seat in one length and plane width.
3. Mark length of each piece according to drawing; saw and plane ends.
4. Construct back and side pieces and finish with back saw, turning saw, knife, and file.
5. Mark out heart-shaped holes and finish with ⅜-inch centre bit, compass, saw, and file.
6. Sandpaper.
7. Locate places for brads and nail parts together.

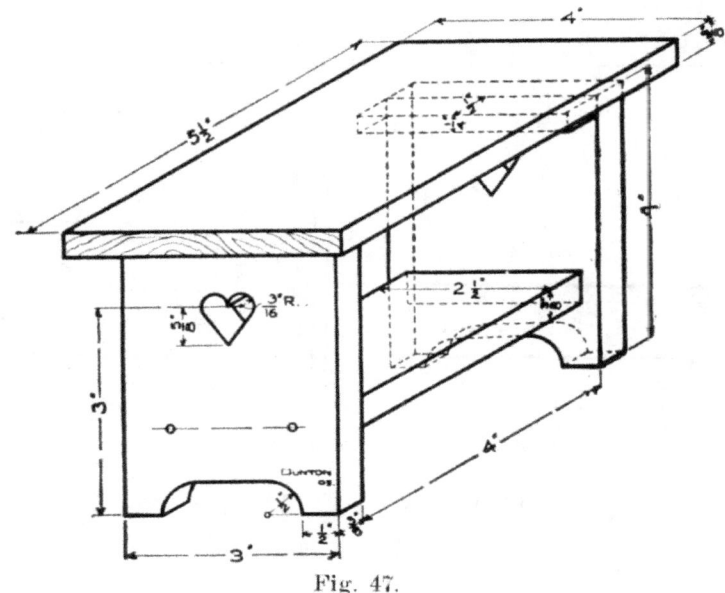

Fig. 47.

DOLL'S TABLE

Whitewood. ⅜ inch.

DIRECTIONS

1. Mark and cut two legs in one length and plane width.
2. Mark length of each piece, saw, and plane.
3. Make top.
4. Prepare shelf and two cleats according to drawing.
5. Construct feet and heart-shaped holes. (See Chair, 4, 5, 6, and 7.)

NOTE: A child's chair and table may be made by using ¾-inch wood and enlarging the dimensions about three times.

In this case 1½-inch No. 9 screws should be used for fastening parts together.

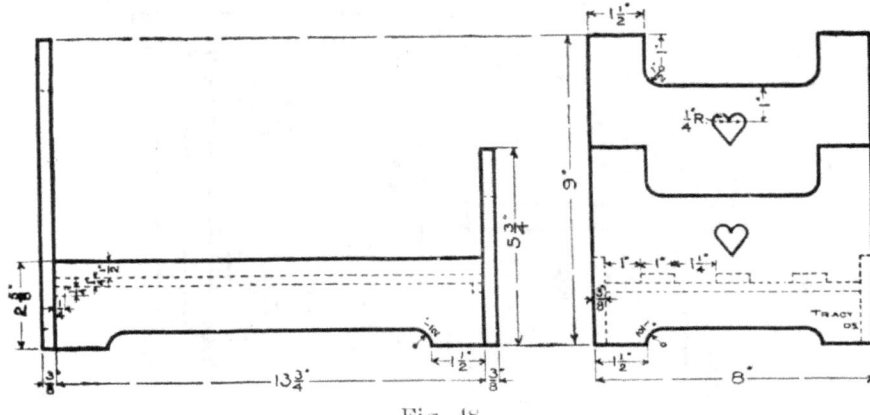

Fig. 48.

DOLL'S BEDSTEAD
Whitewood. ⅜ and ¼ inch.

DIRECTIONS

1. Make the two uprights in one length, plane narrow sides.
2. Mark length, saw, and plane.
3. Make the two side pieces in one width, plane narrow sides and ends, mark width, cut apart, and plane.
4. Construct shape of uprights and sides according to drawing.
5. Finish top of uprights, using 1-inch centre bit at round corners.
6. Construct feet and heart-shaped holes. (See Chair 4, 5, 6, and 7.)
7. Mark out the strips for the bottom and the cleats in one piece 15 x 4 x ¼ inch.
8. Mark and cut pieces to proper dimensions.
9. Sandpaper and fasten parts together.

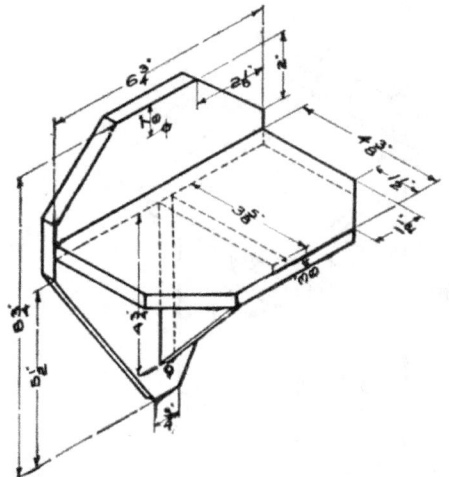

Fig. 49.

SHELF

Whitewood. ⅜ inch.

DIRECTIONS

1. Construct the parts in detail upon paper or blackboard.
2. Let pupil estimate amount of wood required.
3. Take greatest length of parts in the direction of the grain.
4. Construct back, shelf, and bracket according to drawing.
5. Saw and plane parts to given dimensions.
6. Bore holes at top and bottom of back with $\frac{3}{16}$-inch drill bit.
7. Sandpaper parts.
8. Space places for brads or screws and fasten parts together.

NOTE: If screws are preferred, use ¾-inch No. 6. The shelf may be stained and polished.

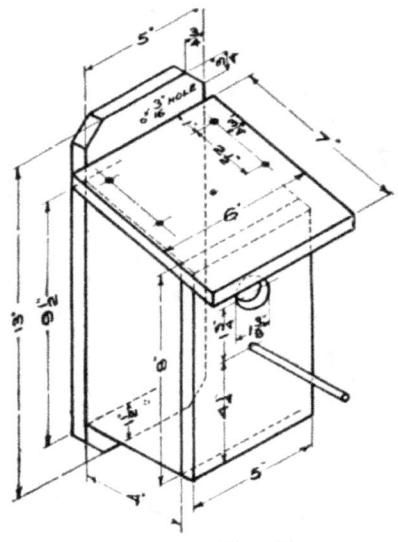

Fig. 50.

BIRD HOUSE
Whitewood. ½ inch.

DIRECTIONS

1. See 1 in model Shelf. Fig. 49.
2. Estimate wood for back and front in one piece and sides and bottom in one.
3. Plane required width of these two pieces.
4. Measure out according to drawing and cut lengths. Plane ends without bench hook.
5. Prepare top.
6. Bore holes for entrance and for ½-inch dowel.
7. Bore four ¼-inch holes through bottom, 1 inch from sides, for drainage.
8. Nail sides together with 1½-inch brads.
9. Fit bottom and top. Nail bottom and fasten top by round head blued screws 1¼ inch No. 8.
10. Insert a dowel 6 x ½ inch.

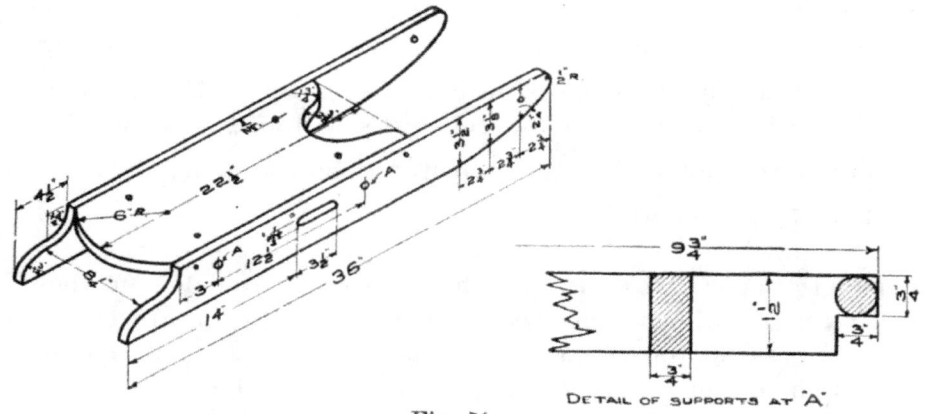

Fig. 51.

SLED

Whitewood or Ash.   ¾ inch.

DIRECTIONS

1. Prepare a piece for the two runners about 36¼ x 7½ inches.
2. Construct the outline of runners and saw with splitting and turning saw.
3. Plane straight sides and use spoke-shave and knife for the curved parts.
4. If convenient, plan for top and the two supports in one piece, about 22¾ x 10 inches. Cut out supports from one side in one length.
5. Plane narrow faces of top and supports to required width.
6. Construct ends on top and support.
7. Use turning saw on curved ends of top and finish with spoke-shave, knife, and file.

ELEMENTARY SLOYD AND WHITTLING

8. Bore a $\frac{3}{4}$-inch hole in a waste piece of wood. Finish round ends of supports with back saw and knife, and fit tight in $\frac{3}{4}$-inch hole.
9. Mark out and bore holes on sides of runners. Finish the handle hole with $\frac{3}{4}$-inch centre bit, compass saw, knife, and file.
10. Bore screw holes with $\frac{3}{16}$-inch drill bit and use countersink.
11. Use $1\frac{1}{2}$-inch screws No. 9.

NOTE: If under part of runners have the edges rounded off, they may be used without iron shoes. If children are able to do so, they may use hoop iron for shoes, punching, drilling, and countersinking holes for screws, bending it around the "toe" and "heel" and fastening with $\frac{1}{2}$-inch No. 6 screws.

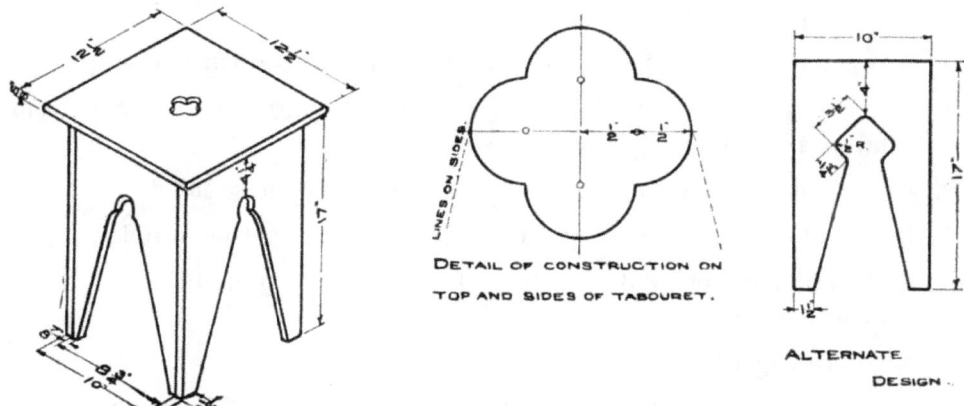

Fig. 52.

TABOURET

Whitewood or Basswood. ⅝ inch.

DIRECTIONS

1. Saw out two pieces of wood for sides, one 34½ x 10¼ inches and the other 34½ x 9 inches.

2. If too long to plane, cut each piece in halves and plane to required width.

3. Plane each end square to required length.

4. Draw construction on each of the four sides and cut with centre bit, splitting saw, knife, and spoke-shave.

5. Smooth inside of each piece with plane and sandpaper.

6. See that the narrow faces of the two narrow sides are perfectly square.

ELEMENTARY SLOYD AND WHITTLING

7. Make four cleats each $7\frac{1}{4} \times \frac{3}{4} \times \frac{3}{4}$ inch and bore two $\frac{3}{16}$-inch holes through both sides.
8. Screw cleats on the inner side of the four pieces flush with top.
9. Space and mark for nails on the two broad sides, about 1 inch from ends and 3 inches between nails.
10. Use $1\frac{1}{2}$-inch brads and drive nearly through at these marks.
11. Put glue on narrow side and nail each corner together quickly.
12. Sink nails, smooth sides with plane and sandpaper, take off sharp corners with sandpaper.
13. Prepare top $12\frac{1}{2} \times 12\frac{1}{2}$ inches.
14. Find centre, construct quarterfoil, and bore with 1-inch centre bit. To avoid splitting bore last hole so that lip and cutter of bit revolve in the direction of the grain.
15. Round narrow faces with plane about $\frac{1}{4}$ inch.
16. Smooth with plane and sandpaper.
17. Fit top on sides and fasten with $1\frac{1}{4}$-inch screws through cleats.
18. Stain with walnut water stain. When dry, sandpaper lightly, polish with wax, and brush and give it a coat of shellac.

In addition to the articles described, a number of simple and useful objects may be designed by teachers and pupils.

STAINING AND POLISHING

GENERALLY it is best to keep the natural color of the wood, especially when the color and the grain have a pleasing appearance.

Some simple stain may be applied on such plain objects as would warrant it, and should be such as not to cover up the grain of the wood like paint. Walnut water stain is most satisfactory. It gives to the wood a dark brown color. If not dark enough, another coat should be applied after the first is dry. If too dark, water should be added. If a green color is wanted, a very small amount of green crystal aniline may be added to the water stain. The mixture, however, should first be tried on a waste piece of wood in order to ascertain if the color is right.

A simple method of polishing may be employed with or without previous staining by applying raw linseed oil and sandpapering lightly until dry. Then rub with soft shavings or cloth.

Another simple method of polishing is to apply "Butchers' Floor Wax" with a piece of cloth, brushing it with a stiff, clean brush as you would polish shoes. Similar wax may be made by mixing beeswax and turpentine to the consistency of soft clay. A coat of thin shellac, quickly and evenly applied with a brush, will make the finish more durable.

WHITTLING

WHITTLING

In the Elementary Sloyd described in the first part of this book, whittling is not practised. As a general rule, children under twelve years of age have not sufficient strength or control of the hand to use the knife correctly. Whittling is recommended only when it is not possible to have the Elementary Sloyd, which requires a special room fitted up with benches and a variety of tools. Such an outfit is more effective educationally, but economically it is more expensive. Whittling can be done in the regular schoolroom by the regular teacher and with a comparatively inexpensive outfit.

By a skilful, experienced, and tactful teacher a whole class of the usual size in the public schools may be instructed simultaneously, but as in any work of motor training, or whenever the hands are employed to give expression to thought, the difference in individuals reveals itself so plainly that it is evident that the best educational results can be obtained only when free scope is given to individual abilities. Consequently, the number of children in the class should be limited. Drill, mass instruction, and various means of keeping children together may be employed and some fairly good visible results obtained, but in nine cases out of ten the educational effect on the child is very little, and in some cases more injurious than helpful. Hence, it is important that in this work a regular class be divided whenever it is possible.

The children should be taught to make sketches and working drawings of the simple models and should also learn to read printed drawings or such as are made by some one else.

The model and the drawing should at first be presented together by the teacher, and enlarged blackboard drawings may be made for the whole class to read. The aim of drawing is to give the pupil a correct mental picture of what he is expected to make, consequently it should always precede manual work.

ELEMENTARY SLOYD AND WHITTLING

The knife is the least mechanical and the most familiar of tools, and if correctly used teaches the pupil to think before he acts, because of its simultaneous demand upon the mind and the muscles of the arm, wrist, hand, and fingers.

The knife, however, is only one among the half hundred cutting tools used in sloyd. The value of Whittling alone as a means of education may not be very great, but it is believed that it may supply an educational need when practised under the following conditions:

1. The child should have sufficient strength to handle the knife correctly.

2. The whittling should be taught preferably by the regular teacher, who must be possessed of sufficient technical skill.

3. The position of the body and the movements used in the various exercises must be such as not to retard physical growth.

4. The work should as much as possible be done in erect standing position and the material should be large enough to permit freedom of movement.

5. The exercises should be carefully graded from the easy to the difficult and should be applied on objects useful to the worker and of artistic merit.

6. The knife should be of correct size and construction.

7. Wood suitable to the objects should be carefully selected and properly prepared.

GENERAL DIRECTIONS

1. With the point of the knife draw and cut in a good sitting position; but whittle, use the sandpaper, bore, etc., in an easy, correct standing position.

2. Always hold the rule on the edge in measuring, marking, and testing for dimensions, and place it flat on material when drawing lines.

3. Keep lead pencils sharp. Adjust the point of pencil to the same length as the point of the compass. In drawing arcs and circles hold compasses at the top between thumb and forefinger and keep needle point as nearly perpendicular to the surface as possible.

4. In squaring lines and testing, hold beam of the try square close to the true face. Whittled surfaces which are less than one-quarter of an inch should not be tested by the try square.

5. Use the eyes to test straightness, squareness, and symmetry of work before applying any other testing instruments.

6. Grasp the knife with the right hand, if right-handed, with the thumb bound over the fingers as in clenched fist.

7. Hold the wood at the end nearest you.

8. Rest forearm against body and cut from you and downward.

9. Do not cut from the very end, but start first beyond the hand, and turn the wood to finish.

10. Try to use the whole length of the blade by drawing it through the wood as you cut. Do not scrape.

11. If you have a broad face to cut, take off the edges first.

12. Never cut clear across an end or the fibres, but always from the sides toward the middle.

13. Do not use sandpaper before the model is as well finished as possible with the knife. Remove pencil marks with an eraser.

14. Stretch sandpaper over a block with the fingers when sandpapering flat surfaces. Remember that the purpose of using sandpaper is merely to make the object clean and smooth and not to reduce dimensions.

WORKING DIRECTIONS FOR WHITTLING

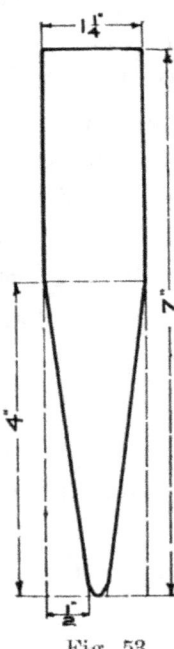

Fig. 53.

1.—PLANT LABEL
Basswood. $\frac{3}{16}$ inch.

DIRECTIONS

Wood sawed off $7\frac{1}{4}$ and split to $1\frac{1}{2}$ inches.

1. Draw a straight line near and parallel to one split edge and whittle to it.
2. Mark width at each end, connect points by a line, and whittle to it.
3. Construct point according to drawing and whittle.
4. Measure length. Square line across and whittle from corners toward centre.
5. Sandpaper with block, narrow faces first, then broad faces.

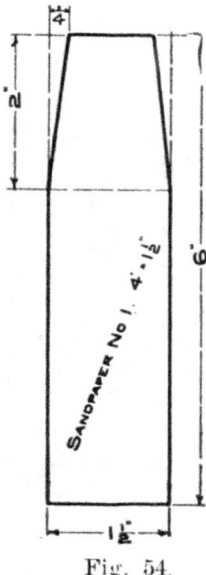

Fig. 54.

2.—PENCIL SHARPENER

Whitewood. $\tfrac{3}{16}$ inch.

DIRECTIONS

Wood sawed off and split $6\tfrac{1}{4}$ x $1\tfrac{3}{4}$ inches.

1. See 1 and 2 in Model No. 1.
2. Square line across near one end and whittle to it.
3. Measure length and draw line and whittle.
4. See 4 in Model No. 1.
5. See 5 in Model No. 1.
6. Mark out on the back of sandpaper a piece the proper size and cut with a knife kept for the purpose.
7. Apply a thin coat of Le Page's Liquid Glue to back of sandpaper and press it firmly upon the wood.

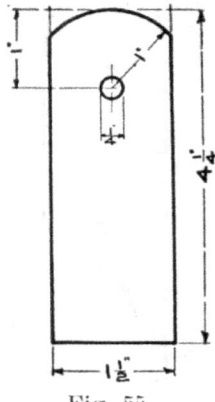

Fig. 55.

3.—KEY TAG

Basswood. $\frac{3}{16}$ inch.

DIRECTIONS

Wood prepared $4\frac{1}{2}$ x $1\frac{3}{4}$ inches.

1. See 1 and 2, Model 1.
2. Locate point and draw arc with compass. Whittle to line.
3. Bore hole at centre with gimlet bit, taking care to keep the bit **perpendicular**. When centre point appears, turn wood and finish.
4. See 4 in Model No. 1.
5. See 5 in Model No. 1.

ELEMENTARY SLOYD AND WHITTLING

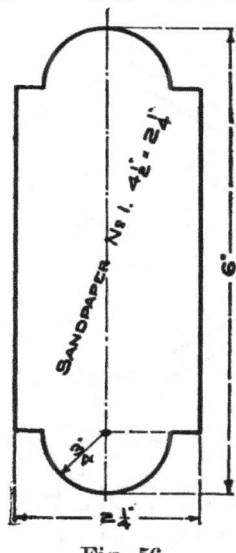

Fig. 56.

—MATCH SCRATCHER
Whitewood. ⅛ inch.

DIRECTIONS
Wood prepared 6¼ x 2½ inches.

1. See 1 and 2, Model No. 1.
2. Draw centre line.
3. Locate points for centres of semicircles at each end, and square lines across at these points.
4. Draw semicircles.
5. Cut square shoulders by notching. Finish to semicircles, taking care to whittle with the grain.
6. Bore hole with fine brad awl at the centres.
7. See 5 in Model No. 1.
8. See 6 and 7 in Model No. 2.

ELEMENTARY SLOYD AND WHITTLING

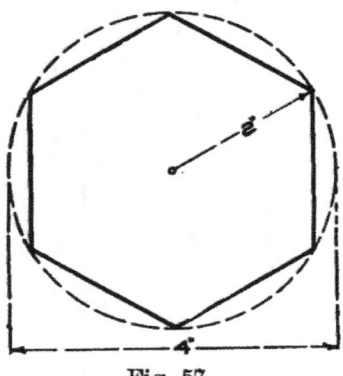

Fig. 57.

5.—STAND FOR PAPER FILE
Whitewood. ¼ inch.

DIRECTIONS

Wood prepared 4¼ x 3¾ inches.

1. Find centre of wood and draw straight line with the grain.
2. Draw a circle of 2-inch radius.
3. Construct hexagon, beginning at the intersection of the centre line.
4. Whittle the two sides running parallel to the grain first, then the others.
5. Draw and cut a bevel of ⅛ inch on the side free from pencil marks and make it round by cutting off sharp edges.
6. See 5 in Model No. 1.
7. For the file use a steel wire brad 4 inches in length No. 14. Sharpen point on the oil stone and drive it through from the under side at centre.

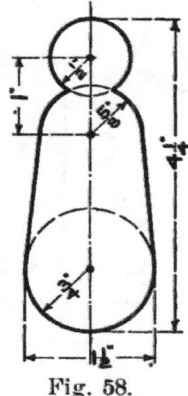

Fig. 58.

6.—TAG
Whitewood. ⅛ inch.

DIRECTIONS
Wood prepared 4½ x 1¾ inches.

1. See 1 in Model No. 5.
2. Locate points for arcs and draw circles.
3. Draw straight lines through tangents.
4. Whittle to straight line first and then to arcs
5. See 5 in Model No. 1.

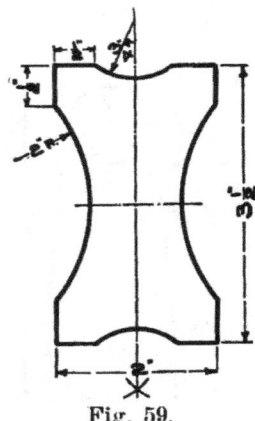

Fig. 59.

7.—THREAD WINDER

Basswood. $\frac{3}{16}$ inch.

DIRECTIONS

Wood prepared $3\frac{3}{4}$ x $2\frac{1}{4}$ inches.

1. See 1 and 2 in Model No. 1.
2. Square line across near one end and whittle to it.
3. Measure length, square line, and whittle.
4. Measure and draw two centre lines, dividing width and length.
5. Mark points for corners.
6. Locate centres for arcs with compasses from these points.
7. Draw arcs and whittle.
8. Sandpaper curves by hand, and straight faces with block.

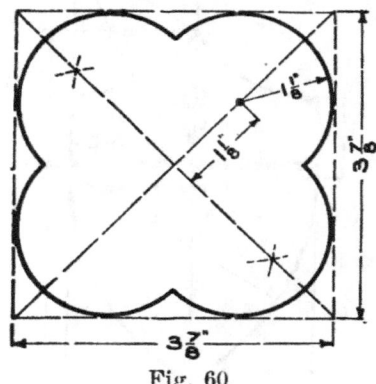

Fig. 60.

8.—MAT
Whitewood. ⅛ inch.

DIRECTIONS
Wood prepared about 4 x 4 inches.

1. Draw one diagonal. Erect perpendicular at centre.
2. Find centre for quarterfoil and construct semicircles according to drawing.
3. Whittle to line, noting carefully the direction of the grain.
4. See 5 in Model No. 1.

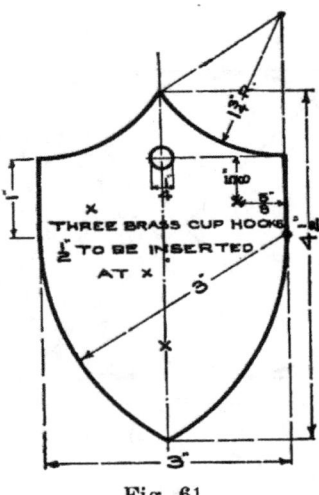

Fig. 61.

9.—KEY BOARD

Whitewood. $\tfrac{3}{16}$ inch.

DIRECTIONS

Prepare wood $4\tfrac{5}{8} \times 3\tfrac{1}{8}$ inches.

1. Make the piece 3 inches wide.
2. Draw a centre line and construct shield according to drawing.
3. See 3 in Model No. 8.
4. Bore hole and mark places for three hooks.
5. Sandpaper.
6. Insert hooks.

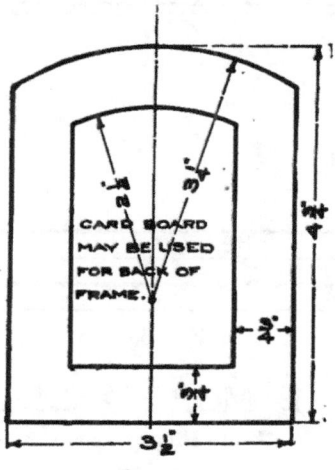

Fig. 62.

10.—PICTURE FRAME
Basswood. ¼ inch.

DIRECTIONS

Size of frame may be decided by pupil with the teacher's approval.

1. Cut two sides and one end square.
2. Draw centre line and construct according to drawing.
3. Place wood firmly on a cutting-board, and with point of knife score and notch lines across the interior about ⅛ inch inside of line until the knife point is through the wood. Cut and score carefully, in a similar manner, the other two sides. Whittle the interior to line.
4. Whittle outer curved end.
5. Sandpaper.
6. The frame may be stained with walnut water stain, and waxed and brushed on the front and narrow faces.
7. Cut cardboard for the back ¾ inch wider and ⅜ inch longer than opening. Cut strips of cardboard ¼ inch wide and glue on three sides of the back of cardboard, and, when dry, glue onto frame, making a pocket for the picture.

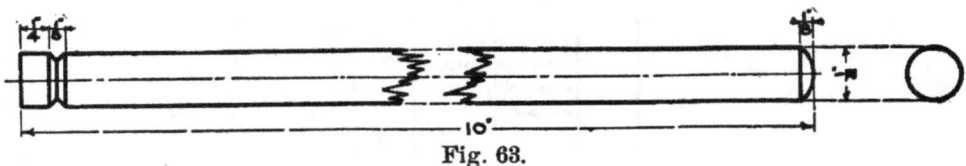

Fig. 63.

11.—MOP HANDLE

White Pine. ½ inch.

DIRECTIONS

Straight-grained wood should be selected about 11 inches long and split about ¾ inch wide.

1. See 1 and 2, Model No. 1. Whittle with long, steady strokes.
2. Whittle edges at both ends until octagonal. This will serve as a guide in cutting the rest of the stick.
3. Cut the next set of corners, making it sixteen-sided, and then cylindrical.
4. Finish one end. Mark and notch around this end according to drawing.
5. Cut length and round the end ⅛ inch, taking care to keep intersection sharp.
6. Sandpaper by hand.

ELEMENTARY SLOYD AND WHITTLING

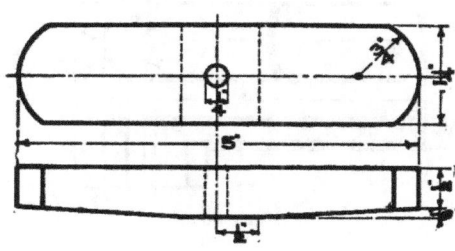

Fig. 64.

12.—DOOR BUTTON
Whitewood.   ⅜ inch.

DIRECTIONS

Prepare wood 5¼ x 1½ inches.

1. Draw lines and whittle two sides straight and square.
2. Mark and draw oblique lines for under part and whittle.
3. Draw a centre line and arcs at both ends and bore hole from both sides.
4. Whittle curved ends.
5. Sandpaper.

(This button may be used for a door which is flush with the casing.)

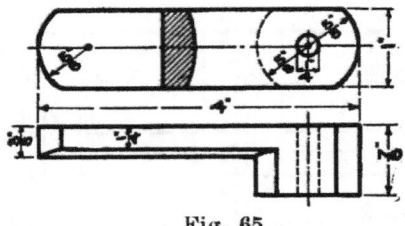

Fig. 65.

13.—DOOR BUTTON
White Pine.   ⅜ inch.
DIRECTIONS
Prepare wood 4½ x 1¼ inches.

1. See 1 in Model No. 12.
2. Construct on the two narrow sides according to drawing.
3. Draw centre line and arcs.   Draw on both sides at thick end.
4. Notch and whittle the thin part of button.
5. Whittle the curved ends and bore hole from both sides.
6. Make the under part of thin end a little curved to avoid friction (see cross section).
7. Sandpaper.

(This button may be used for a door with a moulding.)

ELEMENTARY SLOYD AND WHITTLING

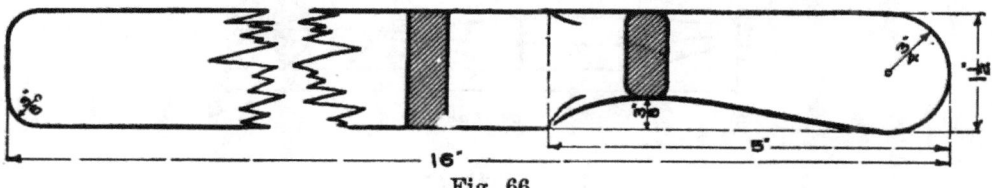

Fig. 66.

14.—BAT FOR TIP CAT
Whitewood. ½ inch.

DIRECTIONS

Prepare wood 16¼ x 1¾ inches.

1. Whittle wood straight and square, making width according to drawing.
2. Construct handle and whittle.
3. Measure and cut length.
4. Draw arc at corners and whittle.
5. Round edges of handle according to drawing.
6. Sandpaper.

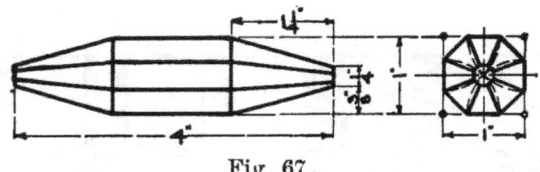

Fig. 67.

15.—TIP CAT
White Pine.   1 inch.

DIRECTIONS
Prepare wood 4¼ x 1¼ inches.

1. See 1, Model 14.
2. Cut one end square, measure length, square line, and cut.
3. Measure and square lines around for pointed ends.
4. Measure and draw ¼ inch square at centre on each end.
5. Draw oblique lines for points on two opposite sides and whittle.
6. Draw and whittle the other sides in a similar manner.
7. Whittle middle part octagonal.
8. Whittle pointed ends octagonal.
9. Sandpaper with block.

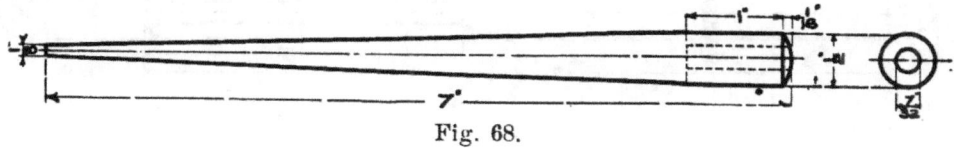

Fig. 68.

16.—PEN-HOLDER

Red Cedar. ¼ inch.

DIRECTIONS

Prepare wood 7½ x ¾ inch.

1. See 1 in Model No. 14.
2. Draw diagonals at one end and bore hole with $\frac{7}{32}$-inch drill bit.
3. Whittle peg and insert before cutting right length. Try if a pen can be easily inserted.
4. Measure and draw oblique lines on one side and whittle.
5. Proceed in a similar way on the other side.
6. Whittle edges, making it octagonal.
7. Whittle next set of edges, making it round.
8. Whittle thick end curved. Measure length and cut.
9. Sandpaper.

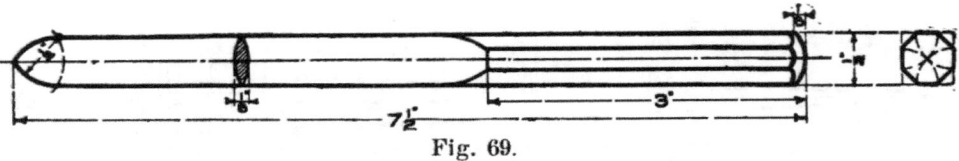

Fig. 69.

17.—LETTER OPENER
Sweet Gum.   ⅛ inch.

DIRECTIONS

Prepare wood 8 x ⅜ inch.

1. See 1, Model No. 14.
2. Mark length of handle and square line around.
3. Draw centre lines on the two opposite planed faces.
4. Draw lines for thickness of blade on each side of centre line.
5. Whittle thickness of blade flat.
6. Whittle handle octagonal.
7. Whittle blade curved to centre lines (see cross section).
8. Cut the curved end of handle.
9. Measure length, draw point of blade, and whittle.
10. Sandpaper octagonal handle with block, blade and ends by hand.

See that blade is sharp enough to cut paper.

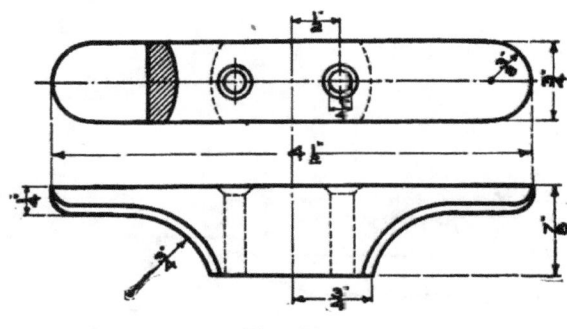

Fig. 70.

18.—LINE CLEAT
Birch. ¾ inch.

DIRECTIONS

Prepare wood 4¾ x 1 inch.

1. See 1 in Model No. 14.
2. Measure length and find middle, square lines around at these marks. Draw centre line on top.
3. Construct side view according to drawing.
4. Cut to these lines, flat.
5. Draw semicircles on top and arcs at bottom.
6. Cut semicircles and curved under part.
7. Bore holes.

NOTE: A variation in shapes and sizes of this cleat may be made. The long sides and top may be curved, making it narrower at ends and more beautiful. The cleat may be used for boats, flag-pole lines, or clothes-line. It is considered better than those made of metal.

ELEMENTARY SLOYD AND WHITTLING

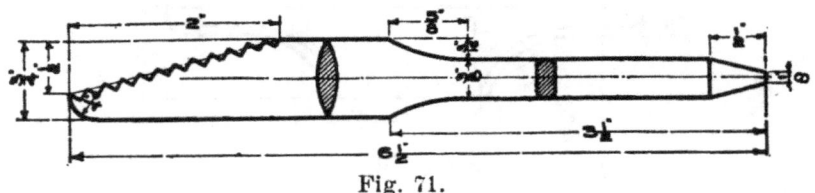

Fig. 71.

19.—CLAY MODELING TOOL
Maple. $\tfrac{3}{16}$ inch. (Straight-grained.)

DIRECTIONS
Prepare wood 6¾ x ⅞ inch.

1. See 1 in Model 14.
2. Mark and cut the required length.
3. Make construction complete on one side according to drawing.
4. Whittle to lines.
5. Model the blade to a sharp edge and round the corners of handle.
6. Cut notches on back of blade, and point the four sides on end of handle.
7. Sandpaper, making the knife edge strong and durable.

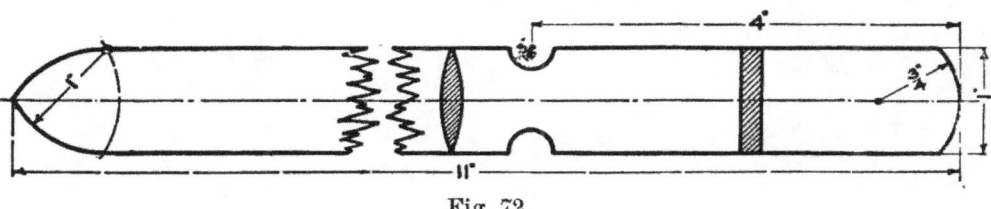

Fig. 72.

20.—PAPER KNIFE

Maple. $\frac{3}{16}$ inch. (Straight-grained.)

DIRECTIONS

Prepare wood 11½ x 1¼ inches.

1. See 1, Model No. 14.
2. Construct knife on one side according to drawing.
3. Whittle to lines.
4. Draw centre lines on narrow faces of blade.
5. Whittle blade curved (see cross section).
6. Sandpaper semicircular cuts by putting sandpaper around the lead pencil, and the rest with block.

WHITTLING OUTFIT

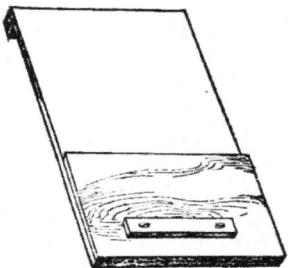

Fig. 73.

DESK TOP FOR WHITTLING COURSE
Regular size, 9 x 15 inches.

Fig. 74.

BOX FOR WHITTLING OUTFIT

This box is designed for a class of twenty in Whittling Course. Contains twenty of each—Lead Pencils No. 3; Rules, one foot; Sloyd Knives, 3-inch blade; New Pencil Compasses, Try Squares 4-inch, Sandpaper Blocks. Price, $15.

ELEMENTARY SLOYD AND WHITTLING

CHEST CONTAINING TEACHERS' TOOLS AND SUPPLIES AS FOLLOWS:

Cross-cut Saw, 22-inch; Try Square, 8-inch; Hatchet No. 1, Clamp Vise; Bit Brace, 2 drill bits, with bit points $\frac{7}{32}$ inch; 6 Auger-bit Gimlets, $\frac{1}{4}$-inch; India Oil Stone, Oil Can, 2 Honing Straps, 2 pounds Cotton Waste, 2 quires Sandpaper No. 0 and No. 1.

AMOUNT OF WOOD FOR THE FIRST TEN MODELS FOR TWENTY PUPILS.

The wood should be of best quality, straight-grain, kiln-dried, and planed.

7 square feet $\frac{1}{8}$-inch Whitewood, approximate width 6 inches.
5 " " $\frac{3}{16}$- " " " " 5 "
3 " " $\frac{1}{4}$- " " " " 8 "
5 " " $\frac{1}{8}$- " Basswood " " 6 "
5 " " $\frac{3}{16}$- " " " " 6 "

If the teacher has no facilities for cutting up the wood, pieces cut to the approximate length and width may be ordered. State kind and thickness as well as number of pieces needed of each kind.

ILLUSTRATION OF SPONTANEOUS CREATIONS

ELEMENTARY SLOYD AND WHITTLING

NAMES OF OBJECTS IN FIG. 75 AS GIVEN BY THE CHILDREN

1. Chain (showing working method).
2. Chain (complete).
3. Dagger.
4. Sword.
5. Wheelbarrow.
6. Pistol.
7. Eyeglasses.
8. Pencil-box.
9. Horse's head.
10. Razor.
11. Hatchet.
12. New York dude.
13. Rocking-chair.
14. "The Old Oaken Bucket."
15. Rolling-pin.
16. Revolver.
17. Ladder.
18. Shovel.
19. Bat and ball.
20. Spade (for greasing axles).
21. Canoe.
22. Row-boat.
23. Clock.
24. Puzzle (made from one piece
25. House with attic.
26. Cuban sword.
27. The pig that swims in the sea.
28. Camel.
29. Doll.
30. Pistol.
31. Catapult.
32. Double-runner.
33. Sled.
34. *Mayflower*.
35. Fulton's boat.
36. Steamboat.
37 and 38. Yoke of oxen with sled.
39. House (made by Thomas Stringer, deaf, dumb, and blind).
40. Saw-horse.
41. Sled.
42. Carpenter's bench.
43. Lumber wagon.

This collection of objects, made without supervision or direction on the part of the teacher, is of special value to those interested in child study. It is suggestive in many ways. The child's imagination, interest, and creative instinct are manifested in these bits of wood, and those who are planning courses of work may "catch some hints" from such productions.

Fig. 75.—Spontaneous Creations in Wood by Children under Twelve Years of Age.

www.ingramcontent.com/pod-product-compliance
Lightning Source LLC
Chambersburg PA
CBHW060422010526
44118CB00017B/2325